COME ON BOARD

GORDON J R SMITH

Tale

COME ON BOARD

Written and produced by the author Gordon J R Smith
Copyright © 2020 Gordon J R Smith

ISBN 978-0-6480386-6-5

National Library of Australia Cataloguing-in-Publication entry:
Creator: Smith, Gordon JR, author.
Title: Come on Board / Gordon JR Smith.

Email gordon.smith9715@gmail.com

Tale Publishing
Melbourne

COME ON BOARD

TABLE OF CONTENTS

PROLOGUE

This book is the story of my voyages on two ocean liners. The *TSS Moreton Bay* in 1951 from Port Melbourne to Southampton, and the *TSS Orion* in 1953 from Naples to Port Melbourne, each very different in duration of voyage, type of ship, accommodation and my experiences onboard each.

One of the voyages I described as being 'absolutely fabulous' and the other 'very troubling.' Never the less, I was very fortunate as a young lad to have had the opportunity to travel on a mode of transport that is sadly not available at the time of writing. Both of which were unforgettable highlights of my long life.

The *TSS Moreton Bay* was a one-class ship of 35,000 tons displacement and a cruising speed of 15 knots. It carried freight and passengers and remained to port long enough to load freight, which usually took two days, but sometimes more. This allowed passengers time to get a feel for the country and its people at most ports of call.

Many of the passengers were about my age of 24 or so, and

were literally embarking on an adventure of a lifetime. They were excited, friendly and enjoying to the utmost life on board, playing card games, drinking and smoking in the lounge bar. It was this air of young conviviality that earned the voyage to Southampton the description of being 'absolutely fabulous,' and prompted the exclamation; "This is really living," to be shouted out many times during the voyage.

The *TSS Orion* was a two-class ship, first and tourist class, of 20,000 tons displacement and 20 knots cruising speed. It was a mail ship and carried no freight, only remaining in port for one day to transfer mail and passengers and some supplies. Both ships were powered by turbines and driven by twin screws, hence the prefix TSS to their names. I will be omitting these prefixes in this manuscript as being superfluous to the narrative.

During WWII both ships in various forms served their country with distinction. Many other ships like the *Moreton Bay* and *Orion* transported thousands of assisted passage migrants to Australia right up until the program ended in 1970, although in the intervening period many of these ships reached the end of their lives and were scrapped.

I was a tourist class passenger and as such was relegated to the stern section of the vessel. The main reason why I called this voyage 'very troubling' was not really to do with the ship and its tourist class passengers of which I was one. It was uniquely personal, stemming from a good turn I did for Dot, an Australian young lady who I met in the Youth Hostel in Naples. Dot told me it was essential that she obtained a passage ticket back to Australia on the *Orion*, but she couldn't get a boarding pass to allow her to get on the *Orion* to purchase a ticket from the purser's office.

Dot asked me to help her. I listened to her devious plan and after giving it much thought, I agreed to help her. Her plan worked and Dot got her tourist class passage ticket back to Australia.

Very soon after the *Orion* left Naples I discovered to my chagrin, that Dot was no 'lady' nor was she as young as me. She attached herself to me and I couldn't get rid of her. Worse still, she was preventing me from making friends with other passengers.

Finally, when I refused Dot's invitation to dance with her, the result was a very dramatic demonstration of the saying: 'Hell has no fury like a woman scorned.' Although all this occurred in the early days of the voyage, it had the effect of destroying my enjoyment of most of the remainder of the voyage. There were also other aspects and happenings of the voyage that troubled me.

There was a stark comparison between the voyage on the *Moreton Bay* and that on the *Orion*. Its passengers of various ages were quite reserved, and the bar service was poor. The food was excellent, but I found the need to report our table steward to the chief steward, because he was treating two young English migrant lads at our table, unfairly. This was very troubling.

There was no recognition when the ship crossed the Equator, (nor in first class I discovered), which I thought would have been a highlight for the assisted migrants that the ship carried, let alone other passengers. The captain was not seen at any time during the voyage, not even at the landfall party. There were a number of functions organized for our enjoyment, race meetings, 'housy-housy' and various dances including fancy dress, some of which I enjoyed. A big disappointment was that the *Orion* only remained in port for one day.

The *Orion* with its yellowish ochre painted hull offset by

white decks, gave the ship a sporty look, while the *Moreton Bay* with its sombre, olive green hull, gave it a more rugged workhorse appearance. Both ships appeared to be well maintained. The tourist class accommodation was on the stern of the *Orion,* where smuts and exhaust products of the ship's chimney could be a problem. First-class passengers up the front in the bow were away from this, but on both ships not at any time on either voyage was the ship's exhaust products of any concern at all.

Describing the voyage on the as 'very troubling' was a very personal opinion, but not I am sure, one that was shared by most of the tourist class passengers who sailed with me, most of whom had joined the ship in Southampton.

CHAPTER ONE
LIFE CHANGING DECISIONS

In 1944 at the age of 17, I began my apprenticeship with the Victorian Railways (VR) as a fitter and turner at the Newport workshops. I completed my apprenticeship in 1949 and became a qualified tradesman fitter and turner. I was earning a full wage and was very happy with life, working for my beloved railways, which I fully expected would be my lifetime vocation.

In the winter of 1946 with the Rover Scouts, I put on a pair of skis for the first time on Mt Donna Buang in Victoria. I was hooked on the sport and my skiing gradually improved over the following couple of winters, skiing on Mt Donna Buang and the Baw Baws in Gippsland. In 1947 and 1948, I stayed at the Rover Scout Chalet for two weeks skiing on the Bogong High Plains in North East Victoria. When I applied for two weeks leave to go skiing again in 1948, I was told that I would not be granted leave in the winter in future. I imagined that this was because I was no longer an apprentice, but was now a tradesman.

Bob Phillips one of the Rover Scouts, said he was a member of the Youth Hostels Association (YHA) and skied with them on weekends at Mt Buller. He suggested I join YHA, saying it was a great club to belong to, Bob said if I came into the YHA club night meeting held each Monday night in the city, he would meet me there.

Back in Melbourne, I went to the YHA meeting, where Bob introduced me to many of the members. I liked what I saw and decided to join YHA right away, never imagining how significant that move would be in determining the exciting path my life would take me in future years.

Life was wonderful, and for some time I had been dating Judy a beautiful blond, YHA member. We were in love, and it was getting serious. However, Judy decided to go abroad, and in 1950 she sailed away to the UK on the *Ugolino Vivaldi* of the Lloyd Triestino Line. I was very sad, but Judy promised to keep in touch while she was away. She did, our letters taking five weeks by ship each way.

After Judy left In 1950, I was invited to join a party of YHA skiers on Mt Bogong the highest mountain in Victoria 6,508 feet (ft). When I returned from that wonderful, sunny week skiing on the mountain, Leon Langley a jovial member of the party, asked me if I would be interested in accompanying him on a working holiday to the UK for about two years.

Leon Langley

I was surprised that he would ask me because, although we had both been members of YHA for some time, we were not close friends. I told Leon that I would have to think about it and would let him know as soon as I had made up my mind.

After Judy left, I dated Lois, a West Australian. I was very fond of her, but soon after we began dating she decided to return to the West. I thought: 'What the hell, why not go to the UK with Leon and follow Judy?' I phoned Leon and told him I was interested in going to the UK with him, but I did not have enough money. I told Leon that if the offer of working for Tom Webb was still possible, I was sure I would be able to earn enough money to go, providing we did not leave for about a year.

Tom Webb was a member of YHA. He had been enticing me to leave the VR and come and work for him and make a lot of money, but I was not interested because I was looking forward to a lifetime career with the VR. However, now my life was about to change, another decision had to be made. I phoned Tom Webb to tell him about Leon's invitation and asked him if the offer of working for him was still available. Tom asked me. "How soon I can you start?" "As soon as I have resigned from the Victorian Railways," I told him.

I went to my VR manager and told him of my intention to go abroad on a 'working holiday' to the UK for two years. I asked for a leave of absence for that period because I wished to resume my employment with the VR when I returned. He told me that this was not possible. This left me with no other option, but to resign, so I resigned there and then.

I wasn't sure what the reaction would be when I told my mother and father. Of course, it was a surprise to them, but they quickly accepted that they would not be seeing their 23 year-old son for about 2 years, which was how long Leon had suggested we would be away. I would never accuse my mother of being a skite, but she certainly got a lot of pleasure telling all her friends that her eldest son Gordon was going abroad to the UK.

I began working for Tom in a small shed at the rear of our

house in Rosanna. The work was on a piecework basis on core dryers for the new Holden car, and it only required the use of a few hand tools. I was soon earning more money than I ever dreamed possible, about £40 each week, compared to about £6 a week as a fitter and turner with the VR!

Leon and I went to a shipping agent in the city, where we paid a deposit and reserved our passages to Southampton on the *Moreton Bay* of the Aberdeen and Commonwealth Line. We were told that the intended sailing date would be in twelve months on the 24th November 1951. That suited me well because it gave me time to earn enough money to pay for the voyage, as well as money to travel to various countries on the Continent and perhaps ski in Austria or Switzerland. I wrote to Judy to tell her when she could expect to see me in London and she wrote back saying she was looking forward to seeing me.

CHAPTER TWO

A BUSY YEAR BEFORE THE VOYAGE

My first encounter with anyone except soldiers who had been overseas was at school when I was ten. Patricia Blackwell a girl in our class at the Heidelberg State School had just returned from a voyage to England. Our teacher asked her to stand up in front of the class and tell us all about England. She told us she had gone to England in a big ship and had seen the King and Queen in their gold coach. The year was 1937 and her parents may have gone to England for the coronation of King George VI.

Empire Day celebration at the school with Patricia as Britannia

The year before she went to England in 1936, Patricia was selected to be Britannia in the Empire Day celebrations on 24th

May. I was one of her page boys. I think that Patricia, who looked very like Shirley Temple without the curls, was my first love. Empire Day was introduced in 1905 to promote loyalty among the Dominion countries of the British Empire and was directed especially at school children. The date of the 24th May was Queen Victoria's birthday. Empire day was discontinued in 1958.

Leon and I obtained our British passports and later had vaccinations against smallpox and some other deadly diseases that we could be stricken with overseas. Without a doctor's certificate stating that we had been vaccinated, we would not have been permitted to leave Australia.

I worked for Tom for seven months and earned just over £600. I ended up with £400 to take away with me because I spent a lot on clothes. I also purchased a good set of golf clubs, complete with bag and shoes, because Tom introduced me to the game of golf and I played a few games with him, which I thoroughly enjoyed nearly as much as skiing. YHA ran a couple of beach and golf trips to Portsea and Torquay. The trip to Torquay was a disaster for me because, just before the trip, I had my vaccinations. Tom had advised me to have these in my buttocks because I would probably not be able to use my arm for work for a few days afterwards.

When I went for the injection the doctor looked at me a little strangely at this request, but when I told him the reason he obliged. I was really looking forward to the game of golf on the Torquay golf course. By the tenth hole, however, I was a cripple, my crotch had swollen up and was hurting like hell. I had to return to the camp, where I spent the rest of the weekend lying down in great pain and having the members sympathize with me in my despair. By Monday my crotch was still sore and swollen a little, but it was not enough to stop me from working and earning big money again.

As well as the YHA beach and golf weekend to Torquay, I went on many YHA hikes and on many weekend work parties to Mt. Buller to help with the building of a YHA hostel on the mountain, so my months of waiting for the voyage to begin were fully occupied by work and YHA activities. Early in November, the shipping agent contacted us, to tell us that the *Moreton Bay* would be leaving Port Melbourne on 25th November at 9:30 p.m. He asked us to come in and pay the balance and pick up our tickets. We were both of course very excited and hurried into the office where the agent gave us our green 'Passage Tickets,' which stated: '*Gordon J R Smith is booked to sail on Voyage 55/H on the steamer TSS Moreton Bay, the intended sailing date to be, on or about November 25th 1951'. My cabin number was 117, berth 3.*' The total fare for the voyage was £68 Sterling.

We were each given two booklets issued by the Aberdeen and Commonwealth Line. The

The front cover of the 24 page information book

24 page larger one, titled *Information for Passengers*, contained just about everything one needed to know about the facilities onboard the *TSS Moreton Bay*. Mealtimes, time zone changes,

sunstroke, medical information, the library and much more. It also listed all the lighthouses, mountains, and many other landmarks normally seen from the ship. Also included was a map of the voyage and ports of call. The book was compiled for the outward voyage from Southampton, but all the information is the same, except that on our inward voyage the ship did not call into Adelaide.

Arriving back home I showed my mother and father and my two

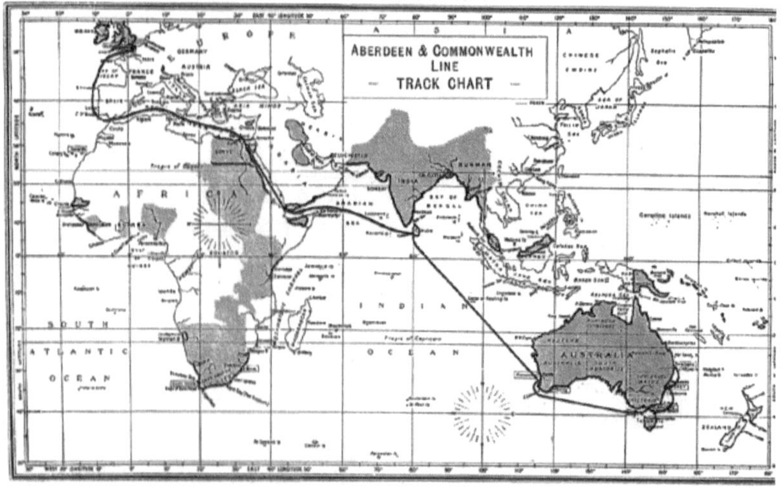

The map in the information book, which I have revised to show the direct route to Fremantle and the port of Ceuta in Spanish Morocco

younger brothers the information books. They were quite excited about my voyage and particularly interested in the map showing the ports the *Moreton Bay* would be visiting. I said I would write a letter and post it if possible at each of the ports.

I learned from the information book that the *TSS Moreton Bay* was a one class ship. This was to have lot to do with my enjoyment of the voyage.

The four page booklet showing the distances and steaming times between ports

The smaller 4 page booklet titled, *TSS Moreton Bay: Distances on outward voyage*, listed all the distances in Nautical miles and steaming times between ports. The booklet stated that a Nautical or sea mile is 6,080 feet, whereas the land or statute mile is 5,280 ft. The times between ports were based on a steaming speed of 15 knots 15 miles/hr. (27.75 km/h). We thanked the agent and he wished us *Bon Voyage.*

In the days leading up to the 25[th.] I packed and said farewell to most of my friends and relations. I also visited the Newport railway workshops where I served my apprenticeship to see my mates and tell them I was going abroad. They wished me luck. On the Monday night before we left, Leon and I went into YHA club night in the city to say goodbye to all our friends. Everybody wished us well, some saying they were already booked on ships to follow us, early in the New Year. Before we farewelled all our friends, many addresses were exchanged for a meeting in the UK, I decided to join up as a life member of YHA. It was a very reasonable fee and I am still a member.

CHAPTER THREE
A LAST ITS SAILING DAY

On the evening of Sunday 25th November 1951, I set off with my family in my brother Donald's old Vauxhall car to Port Melbourne pier. It was a warm, balmy, night and everyone helped me to get my luggage aboard the *Moreton Bay*, a large ship looking spick and span in olive green with cream trimmings. My luggage consisted of one large case, one small case, my rucksack and golf clubs. Leon arrived with his family and there were introductions all round.

There to see me off were my mother and father, my mother looking rather sad, my brothers Geoff and Donald, my uncle and auntie, my

The author's family and relations on board to wish us bon voyage.

father's mother, my cousin Valerie and her boyfriend, John.

Along the length of the ship, there were lines of streamers of all colours joining the ship to the wharf, and more were being thrown out all the time. By now it was nearly dark and the ship's lights, together with those on the wharf were lighting up the ship and streamers making it a grand and exciting sight.

A steward showed us to our cabin and bunks. Leon and I were sharing a four-berth cabin. I took the top bunk of one of the pairs, as Leon said he would like to have a bottom bunk. Then everyone came aboard to have a tour of the ship, and a look at our cabin and bunks.

The streamers between ship and wharf as they looked early in the evening

Around 8:30 p.m. everybody except the passengers were ordered off the ship. I said goodbye to my family with hugs and kisses and told my mother not to worry, I would be OK. We yelled out to each other across the gap even though it was hard to hear with everyone else doing the same with their families and friends.

As the scheduled time for leaving passed by, there was no sign of any movement.

Leon and the author on board just before the Moreton Bay sailed

Members of the crew said freight was still being loaded and our departure would not be delayed much longer. I didn't know that the *Moreton Bay* carried freight: I thought it was only passengers. This delay was the result of the ship's dual-purpose

However, I was to discover that because the *Moreton Bay* earned a portion of its revenue by carrying both freight and passengers, this was a boon to its passengers. It meant that the ship had to stay long enough in ports to load freight, which gave passengers time to learn about the countries and its people that greatly increased the enjoyment of the voyage and that this delay was one of its effects.

As the time moved on toward 10.30 p.m. I began to suffer from one of the worst stomach aches I had ever had. I tried to ignore it. Leon and I kept up a conversation, while waving to our families, who we were sure, were getting heartily sick of waiting, and hoped we would be leaving soon.

I was particularly sorry for my mother that saying farewell to her eldest son had developed into such a long, drawn-out, parting. The streamers were not the same spectacular sight as they had been earlier, they were all looking rather bedraggled, and many had already broken. About 11:30 p.m. the ship's whistle sounded and things began to happen, as we watched the crew carrying out various tasks ready for casting off. At last, the *Moreton Bay* began to move ever so slowly away from the wharf and the link with the mainland and my family was finally broken and the last of the streamers parted.

CHAPTER FOUR

AN ABSOLUTELY FABULOUS VOYAGE BEGINS

PORT MELBOURNE TO FREMANTLE

Distance: 1,655 Nautical miles. Steaming time: 4 days

Monday 26th November: When we woke in the morning, we were at once aware of the movement and noises of the ship. The cabin steward gave us some special soap and told us that only saltwater was available for showering and washing. That was a surprise because it was not mentioned in the information booklet. We had our showers, which weren't too bad, but certainly not as enjoyable as with freshwater. After we had showered and shaved, we went up on deck to find that the *Moreton Bay* was still in sight of land in the far distance on the starboard (right) side of the ship.

We were told we were looking at the Otway Ranges, rising behind Lorne and Apollo Bay. This was an area that was very familiar to Leon and me because we had visited there many times with YHA. It was quite fitting that this was to be the last we would see of the Australian mainland until after we crossed the Great Australian Bight. The next land we would see would be the southernmost point of Western Australia, near Albany.

The ship was rolling gently as we walked around the deck

before going down to the dining room for breakfast. Seated at our table were other young Aussies and we introduced ourselves over a good hearty breakfast.

As the ship headed towards the Great Australian Bight, the weather began to get colder and the wind whipped up the waves. I spent a lot of time on deck, as I was fascinated by watching the waves pass by. I was not troubled by the movement of the ship until later when the seas increased to much larger swells, causing the *Moreton Bay* to pitch and roll quite a lot. It was only when I went down to the dining room that I sometimes felt a little nauseous. The ship was moving so much that table edge boards called 'fiddles' had to be fitted to prevent the plates sliding off the table, which was great fun to experience for the first time.

I decided to try and beat the sick feeling, by taking my plate and cutlery up to the fresh air on the deck, where I ate in a sheltered spot with no trouble. The Chief Steward walked by and said: "If you feel sick eating your meal in the dining room, it will help if you always have one or two beers before meals." I thanked him and did not hesitate to take his advice for the remainder of the voyage, even though the sea might be dead calm.

Although it was quite rough steaming across the middle of the Great Australian Bight, I enjoyed the experience immensely, as neither Leon nor I were really seasick and drinking a beer or two before dinner certainly was the right thing to do. I had never seen the ocean so very blue as it was in the Bight, an indication of how deep the sea was that we were steaming across.

It brought to mind a very, jolly song I heard on the radio many times, but I could only remember the first line: *'A life on the ocean wave. A home on the rolling deep.'* This song and the little I could remember of the words of the rest of the song, painted a picture of how wonderfully exciting and thrilling it was to be a passenger on the *Moreton Bay,* especially now that having a beer or two before dinner had conquered any feelings of nausea I had in the first day or two.

I got quite a fright a couple of times when there was a loud thud and the ship shook a little. A member of the crew told me not to worry: "What I was hearing and feeling was the hull of the ship being supported on the crests of two or more large waves, then dropping into the troughs. I was also hearing the noise of the propellers as they came above the water level and raced, before becoming submerged again." Because the *Moreton Bay* was a one-class ship we could walk around and circumnavigate the whole ship from stem to stern, a definite aid to the enjoyment of the voyage, which was to be our home for the next five weeks.

I gradually got used to life on board and the saltwater ablutions. As I was to discover on my first tour in Austria, some people pay big money in spa resorts to have saltwater treatments for various ailments. We received this treatment each day for nothing! The weather became warmer and the seas less rough as we rounded the southern tip of Western Australia near Albany and steamed up the coast to Fremantle.

Saturday 1st December. The *Moreton Bay* was assisted by a tug to berth in Fremantle Harbour, my first visit to the West of Australia. It was a fine sunny day. We were to stay in port for two days while the ship was loaded with freight.

This was one of the advantages of travelling on a combined freight and passenger vessel, compared to a mail carrying ship. We had to change our watches to Fremantle time, the first of many time changes during the voyage.

Sadly, some passengers were so seasick and incapacitated as the *Moreton Bay* crossed the Bight that they were forced to abandon their voyage in Fremantle. We never did find out what they did, but what a tragic disappointment it must have been for them to only get as far as Fremantle. I wondered if they got a refund, I hoped so.

A tug getting ready to escort our ship into Fremantle Harbour

The information booklet listed details of flights around the various capitals of Australia. For example, a flight from Perth to Melbourne cost £19.11 and took 11 1/2 hours. Air travel around Australia and overseas was a fast but expensive way to travel. People were flying with Qantas to the UK and thence to Helsinki for the 1952 Olympic Games. We hadn't met any passengers so far who came from Adelaide. They would have had to fly or catch *The Overland* train to Melbourne to board the *Moreton Bay* there.

When I got off the ship I rang my former girlfriend Lois, who had returned to West Australia. I had kept in touch with and told her about our voyage. Lois said that we must come and visit her, and she invited Leon and me out to her place for dinner. Before we went to see Lois, we explored Perth, a very attractive, uncrowded city. Later I went and met a Rover Scout friend Ian Howard, who was a trainee surgeon at the Royal Perth Hospital. Ian, of course, got a surprise to see me in Perth. We spent about an hour together reminiscing about all that had happened since we last saw each other. It was a great reunion.

Leon and I took a bus to Lois's beautiful house in the north of Perth. Her father ran a building company. I reckoned that they were quite wealthy. We had a freshwater, hot shower there, which was much more refreshing than the saltwater showers on our ship, but not being aware of how to turn on and off modern shower taps, I nearly scalded myself, because I couldn't turn off the hot tap.

Lois and her charming mother put on a very tasty meal for us. It was a very happy occasion and we never stopped talking as we all had a lot to tell each other. Lois and her parents were particularly interested in how we liked our voyage across the Great Australian Bight. We told them it took five days, and that I suffered from a little nausea at first, and the beer cure, which caused a bit of a giggle, but mostly how we both were thoroughly enjoying the experience of our ship ploughing through the large waves with volumes of spay coming away from the bow. We told them too, how a couple of lady passengers couldn't carry on with the voyage because they were so seasick. It was very pleasing meeting Lois's parents, and I am sure they enjoyed our visit.

When we returned to the ship, we learned that there had been trouble between the crew and the Chief Purser. The Chief Purser had to lock himself in his office because one of the crew wanted to take a knife to him. The police and the Master at Arms finally sorted out the problem, but we never did discover the cause, or if anyone was charged.

During our second day in port, Leon and I took a bus tour organized by the purser, to King's Park on the beautiful Swan River, then to the surf beaches of Cottesloe and Scarborough, to the north of Fremantle. The surf beaches were certainly as good as we had heard from YHA members from Perth, who were always bragging about how their surf beaches were miles ahead of ours in Victoria. We had to admit that the two beaches we visited had beautiful sandy beaches and excellent surf. In the afternoon there was extensive rain with thunder and lightning.

Because of the thunder and lightning, which caused the loading to be suspended, we were told that the ship would spend an extra day in Fremantle to complete loading. I rang Lois to see if we could meet again, and maybe bring her down to see the *Moreton Bay*. She was working, but did not offer to meet me after work, so the last contact I had with her was that phone call, where we said our goodbyes. Lois asked me to write and tell her about my travels. I said I would. I had no deep regrets about the way our relationship ended because I was embarking on a grand new adventure.

There was, however, a sequel to the letters I sent back to Lois. I wasn't aware that she did a stint on a Perth radio station, and discovered later that some sections of the letters I had sent her were being used in a travel program she was putting to air. I am not sure if my name was mentioned. Lois never told me about this in any of her letters to me: However, when I returned to England after my first tour, I stopped writing to her.

Since we were going to have an extra day in port and were not scheduled to leave until 4 p.m., I decided I had time for a game of golf. I managed to get my golf clubs out of the baggage room and played a game at the Fremantle public golf course, which I had seen from the bus. The storms had gone away and I had an interesting game of golf on a fairly rough and ready course. On the way around, I saw plenty of West Australian wildlife. The course was inhabited by many lizards and goannas, but they didn't interfere with the pleasure of my game, and I had a reasonably good score.

Bringing my golf clubs with me was certainly a good idea, coupled with another item I packed, my dinner suit. Not too many backpackers, or for that matter tourists going abroad in those days would take those with them. However, I never regretted including them in my luggage. Both got a lot of use.

During the three days we spent in West Australia and visited two of its principal cities, surf beaches and countryside, I felt I had obtained a good feeling of what it was like to live there so far from our home in Melbourne. I likened Fremantle to Geelong and Perth to Bendigo in our home state of Victoria.

I posted a letter to my family about the voyage across the Bight and how I was a little nauseous, but soon got over that and wrote a little about Perth and Fremantle assuring them that I was well and enjoying the voyage. Leon had a good sense of humour and we were getting on well together.

⚓

FREMANTLE TO COLOMBO

Distance: 3,136 Nautical miles. Steaming time: 8 days 17 hours.

Tuesday 4th December: The *Moreton Bay* pulled up its anchor and cast off the lines and we were on our way to Colombo. There were not many people on the wharf or streamers waving us goodbye. After leaving Fremantle, we settled down to life on board, gradually getting to know the other Aussie passengers about our own age. The majority came from New South Wales, but there were a couple from Adelaide and one from Perth. There were also two girls from New Zealand and one American. Leon and I joined in with this happy group of girls and blokes, who had virtually commandeered the starboard (right) side of the B deck lounge bar, to drink and play cards. All drinks including beer and cigarettes were custom free, so we drank and smoked freely, but I must say never in excess.

The main card game being played was canasta. I did not have a clue how to play the game initially, but after watching them play for a few days, Leon and I were invited to join the group, and we learned quickly how to play the game. I found canasta to be a fascinating card game, and we played on and off all the way to Southampton. It was great fun.

I thought that the trouble between the crew and the Chief Purser in Fremantle had been resolved, but a day or so after leaving Fremantle, I witnessed an incident that caused me to think otherwise. I followed a dining room steward, who was carrying an armful of plates and cutlery, out of a side door that I thought led to the main deck. The door, however, led to a short open deck walkway between the dining room and the galley. To my surprise, the steward suddenly threw all the plates and cutlery over the railing into the sea! Turning to me he said: "That's one for us against the Aberdeen and Commonwealth Line!" He then disappeared into the galley. God knows how much of the *Moreton Bay*'s cutlery and other equipment went to the bottom of the sea. I should have reported him to the Chief Steward, but didn't. I don't know why because I hate waste.

On the port (left) side of the B deck lounge, there were a number of middle-aged couples returning to England. They evidently did not find Australia to their liking. They spent most of the time sipping their drinks, talking, playing cards and other games, and by the nature of their unapproving glances cast across at us, I don't think they liked our young group, who were having such a happy time.

As we talked, drank, smoked and played canasta with the members of our happy young group, we gradually discovered their reasons for travelling to the UK on the *Moreton Bay*. Some, like me, were looking for adventure and travel in the UK and the Continent, and to find out how people lived on the other side of the world. A few were visiting relatives in England and combining this with travel around the British Isles. None were members of YHA, in Australia or New Zealand.

Watching the albatross and flying fish

After steaming across the Indian Ocean for a few days the weather gradually became warmer. We enjoyed sunbathing and playing deck games. We were all acquiring healthy tans, and a few became a little sunburnt. The Captain filled the swimming pool with seawater, which by this time was a lovely refreshing temperature, so swimming was another enjoyable pastime. Steaming across the ocean on a ship like the *Moreton Bay,* I was sure must the most relaxing method of travel possible, with the bar handy, and with the company of such a fun-loving group of young people.

One day the ocean took on a glassy look except for smooth, one, or two metre (m) swells with crests nearly 100 m apart. In these conditions, it was very relaxing and soothing to sit sipping a drink while looking out through the open doors on the other side of the lounge. One minute all that could be seen was sky, and then nothing but ocean, as the *Moreton Bay* lazily rolled from side to side. Another day, when the surface of the water was rather choppy, we watched flying fish. Groups of these fish emerged from the wave crests and flew, or more correctly glided with outstretched small fins just above the surface, then disappeared under the water, only to quickly reappear. They put on a fascinating display nearly all the way to Colombo. Albatross were also keeping us company from time to time, but no dolphins were to be seen.

It was night when we passed the Cocos Islands, so we didn't get a chance to see them. It was off these islands in 1914 that the HMAS *Sydney* engaged the German cruiser *Emden*, which was badly crippled and driven ashore on North Keeland Island on 9th November 1914.

One day early in our voyage on the way to Colombo in the huge Indian Ocean, an officer came into the lounge and announced to our group that: "Captain Milne would like to invite a few of you up to the bridge to take over the helm of our ship for a short while. Is anyone interested?" Up shot a few hands, mine included.

I was selected with about four other blokes to follow the officer up the stairs to the bridge. The view forward of the bridge was spectacular with the front of the ship pitching up and down as it cut through the waves. It was really very exciting to see. Captain Milne greeted us. He was a fair-headed, robust looking man with a pleasant smile. While each of us waited for our turn at the wheel, the captain showed us around the bridge with its compasses, maps and other devices, which was so very interesting to see.

My turn soon came and under the instruction of the helmsman, I took hold of the big wooden helm wheel of the *Moreton Bay* The method of steering a ship, I learned, was first to watch the compass in front of the helm. If the ship deviated from the set heading, the helm was turned the opposite way. The ship invariably swung too far the other way, so another adjustment of the helm was required. This procedure was repeated until the ship settled on to the correct heading. As soon as it deviated again, the correction process was started anew. The sensation of the ship responding to my turn of the helm was absolutely thrilling. When my time at the helm was up, the helmsman told me to look behind the *Moreton Bay* at my wake. It was anything but straight, looking more like a slalom course, but it was very exciting to have control and steer the *Moreton Bay* for that short distance across the Indian Ocean. I don't think present-day backpackers get a chance to pilot a 747 even for a short distance on their way to the UK.

On the way back to the lounge, still thrilled by the experience of steering the ship and being on the bridge, one of the blokes yelled out: "THIS IS REALLY LIVING" and with that, the others joined in, and it sure was. Unknown to Leon and me at the time this exclamation originated from some young people who boarded the *Moreton Bay* in Sydney. They were a happy band of young blokes and girls and whenever an especially exciting event occurred, they yelled out these words. This was the first time I had heard it, but it was to be the cry of joy throughout the voyage all the way to Southampton when there was an event of merit.

As well as some other passengers being invited to have a turn at steering the ship during the voyage, every passenger, in turn, was invited to dine at Captain Milne's table, and my invitation soon came. It was a very convivial dinner, the food was delicious. Seated at the table was a mixture of young and middle-aged passengers, most of whom I had never seen before, not surprising, considering the *Moreton Bay* was a single class ship with some 500 passengers on board.

There was plenty of lively and interesting conversation at the table. The Captain told us some of the history of the *TSS Moreton Bay*. She was built in 1921–22 by Vickers Ltd, at Barrow, England. She has twin screws driven by geared turbines, hence the TSS before her name. Her two sister ships were the *Esperance Bay* and *Jervis Bay*. All three he said were converted into armed merchant cruisers in 1939, and in 1941 the *Moreton Bay* and *Esperance Bay* were converted into troopships, continuing in this role until the end of the war.

There was always something of interest to see, even out in the middle of the Indian Ocean. One of these was watching slightly faster ships pass us by. One day the smoke from a ship could be seen on the horizon, and during the day it gradually drew nearer. The next morning it would be just behind us, then soon in the day, the ship would very slowly pass us at a distance of about a kilometre. Signals would be exchanged between the two ships by Aldus lamp, and no doubt also by wireless. By the next morning the ship would be halfway to the horizon and the next day only a wisp of smoke could be seen near the horizon. Most of these ships passing us were city class freighters, such as the *City of New Orleans,* and the *City of Los Angeles.* I had seen advertisements for this shipping line in *Time* magazine. They were one of a class of ships that were called 'Liberty' ships, which the American ship yards turned out at a fast rate to replace English merchant ships sunk during the war.

Wednesday 7th December: At last the big day of the crossing of the Equator arrived. By now we were swimming regularly in the pool, the saltwater getting warmer and warmer as we steamed north. The crew set up a big log across the swimming pool. This was for us to play games of knocking each other off the log into the pool with stuffed bags, which was great fun. Other games were organized and everyone joined in, which was one advantage of a single class ship.

Later one of the crew came out dressed as Father Neptune, and the 'formal' part of the ceremony got underway. With great hilarity, Neptune inducted each of us into his Kingdom. Our faces were covered in lather and Neptune or one of his helpers shaved

The slippery log

us with a blunt wooden knife, after which our heads were dunked in a large bucket of water. There were many screams from the girls because they were treated in the same manner as the blokes. We were then given a certificate of entry into Neptune's Kingdom. Sadly I have no photo of the occasion and no longer possess the certificate, a relic of travel by sea for which the modern-day airline passenger does not qualify.

After the *Moreton Bay* sailed north past the Equator, I was looking forward to observing an interesting phenomenon, watching the water drain out of the bath in an anti-clockwise direction, instead of clockwise as in the Southern Hemisphere. The wind direction around weather systems would also reverse, but that would not be so readily apparent to us. Sometime after the crossing ceremony, I went below and part filled a bath with water and pulled the plug to see how the water went down the plughole. The bathwater, I reckon, should have gone straight down, but instead, it maintained its clockwise direction! I decided to do a check of the bathwater every couple of days, but there was no change before we reached Colombo.

The weather was sunny for the entire six days of the relaxing voyage between Fremantle and Colombo. The seas were relatively smooth, disturbed only by long, low, swells. On occasions the wind caused the surface to rough up, but nothing more than a pleasant rolling and pitching of the ship. Nothing, in short, prevented us from thoroughly enjoying ourselves, as we swam and played in the pool, sunbathed drank and 'canastered' our way to Colombo the capital of Ceylon, where we were to spend two days, my first-ever visit to a foreign country.

Thursday 13th December: The *Moreton Bay* dropped anchor about 300 m from the wharves in Colombo's harbour in the early morning. Straight away we noticed the heat and humidity. We also noted peculiar, but not unpleasant smells, together with a mystical sunlit haze that covered the land. I had learnt a little about Ceylon in school, how tea was grown in the hills, and also about the Temple of the Tooth in Kandy, so this island, roughly the size of Tasmania was not completely unknown to me.

Motor launches were used to ferry passengers to the Colombo wharves. Most of our group decided to catch a bus for the 15 km around the bay drive from Colombo to Mt Lavinia, a beach tourist resort, once the residence of the Governor of Ceylon We got our free launch tickets from the purser and away we went.

Surprisingly, the bus to take us to Mount Lavinia, was a red double-decker, which enabled most of us to get up on the top deck to see everything around us, as the bus threaded its way through all manner of vehicles, oxen and donkey-drawn carts, cars, bicycles, lots of people, and even a few elephants. Along the road to Mount Lavinia as with the means of transport, the homes were a motley of styles. Mostly they were small shacks, but dotted along the way were substantial modern houses, especially as we neared Mount Lavinia, and in the near suburbs of Colombo. We were enthralled by it all, so different to what we were accustomed to.

The Mount Lavinia beach resort

An oxen drawn cart seen on the way to Mt Lavinia

There was a lovely beach at the Mt Lavinia resort, but none of us had brought our togs. We went into the hotel located on a rocky shelf overlooking the beach and sat down to drinks and tasty salad meal with fried fish. We felt like millionaires as the resort waiters saw to our every need. The cry of: "THIS IS REALLY LIVING" rang out. Leon and I, of course, joined in because it really was so exciting and special. The resort was luxurious, very modern and attractive with cane furniture much in evidence.

We returned on the bus to the Galle Face Hotel, where just outside we saw a snake charmer at work with a cobra. We gave him a few shillings, but I wasn't greatly impressed, because there seemed to be no element of danger about the performance. The Galle Face Hotel is a large colonial-era building with huge fans slowly revolving in the ceiling. We sat in cane chairs and were served with drinks by black waiters. It reminded me of scenes from colonial style movies, but this was the real thing. This time we gazed at each other saying quietly once more: "This is really living" as it surely was.

The snake charmer

Gully Gully boats

The heat and humidity were taking some getting used to. I was sweating like the proverbial pig, or as I was corrected many years ago. 'Horses sweat, men perspire and women glow.'

After lunch, we went into the centre of the city of Colombo, which was very hot, dusty and dirty. We looked at the shops and the stalls, which were selling all manner of wares, carvings, fabrics, clothes and the like. We were followed around by

Singhalese men trying to entice us into various shops with the promise of a good deal. We had been warned never to buy anything at the set price, but always to bargain with the vendor, which we did. Nearly everyone I saw, especially in the city, both men and women, chewed betel nuts, leaving them with horrible red teeth and mouths.

We returned to our ship by launch and joined other passengers leaning over the rails watching the gully gully boats below. These small boats were filled with wares to sell to the passengers on board ships in the port. The trading was carried out with much shouting and yelling as passengers and vendors bargained over items for sale. Goods were either thrown aboard, or attached to long sticks for inspection. When a sale was made, the money was sent back in bags on the sticks. It was an interesting and amusing process, but I found nothing I wanted to buy in Colombo or from the gully gully boats.

Leon and I booked for a tour to the Temple of the Tooth in Kandy. Early the next morning we were on our way in a convoy of four coaches to Kandy, which I had learned about in school, as well as about the 'black hole of Calcutta.' The coach took us along roads crowded just like the day before. We crossed many rivers and streams where women could be seen washing clothes by slapping them on the rocks. The country became very lush and green as we drove steadily inland and the temperature and humidity dropped a little. The coaches gradually gained height, but I didn't see any tea plantations. I believe they were further north in the mountains.

After a journey of some 40 km, the coaches arrived at Kandy, 488 m above sea level. We joined a guided tour, following the guide through a lovely garden to the pink coloured Buddhist Temple of the Tooth. The temple is surrounded by a

The Temple of the Tooth

moat and had pagodas and a high gabled roof.

The guide took us into the dimly lit temple, where we saw a jewel-encrusted, gold casket containing a sacred relic claimed to be Buddha's right eye-tooth. Every August a replica of the tooth is paraded around the city amid huge celebrations.

Around the temple there were many pathetic looking beggars, some I thought afflicted by leprosy. This was in stark contrast to the many well-fed Buddhist monks, resplendent in their vivid orange saris. This fascinating tour took nearly all day. We returned to hot and steamy Colombo for a last look around the city before catching the launch back to our ship.

The TSS Moreton Bay at anchor in Colombo harbour

I thoroughly enjoyed the sights and sounds of Colombo and Ceylon, recalling some of the things I had learnt at school. This experience was certainly an eye-opener for me. As well as observing a new culture and way of life, everything about Ceylon was a surprise, the various novel modes of transport used by the people, together with the towns and villages where they lived, and of course the very hot and humid weather. Both here in Colombo and in Fremantle and Perth we were enjoying the very great advantages of sailing on a freight-carrying ship, which allowed us to explore our first two ports of call and some of the country and people.

In a letter to my family I posted in Colombo, I told them about crossing, the Equator, and about the wonderful happy group of young people I was travelling with, together with a few words about the trip to Mount Lavinia and the Temple of the Tooth.

⚓

COLOMBO TO ADEN

Distance: 2,092 Nautical miles. Steaming time: 5 days 19 hours.

Saturday 15th December: The *Moreton Bay* raised anchor and left Colombo in the evening, leaving behind a beautiful hazy red sky. When I woke the next morning, we were steaming across the Arabian Sea towards Aden. It was a great relief to be away from the heat and humidity of Ceylon. We swam in the pool many times during the day, aware that the water pumped into the pool from the sea was getting warmer each day.

By now we all knew each other and joined in the games on board, having great fun. The blokes and girls from Sydney were the life of the voyage, and many happenings brought about the exclamation of "THIS IS REALLY LIVING!"

I was having so much fun that it wasn't until the second day out from Colombo on the way to Aden that I remembered to look at the bathwater to see if the direction of the emptying water had changed. I half-filled the bath and let the water drain out while watching the plug hole intently. Lo and behold, the direction of the water vortex going down the plughole at last had reversed direction to anticlockwise.

I went up to the bar to have a beer and tell the group what I had discovered. Most of them looked at me a bit stupidly from the canasta game they were playing, but a couple of the blokes understood what I had witnessed. I explained to our group about the winds around the weather systems, which would change direction as well. However, they all went on with their drinking, smoking and playing canasta that was much more important than any rotation of emptying bathwater!

One of my favourite forms of relaxation was to walk along the deck to the stern of the *Moreton Bay*; which being a one-class ship, meant that every passenger had the use of all the deck space. I would look over the railing and watch the wake trail behind the ship, not this time in the shape of a slalom course, but straight, under the control of the ship's expert helmsmen. Sometimes the sea level would be nearly up to the railing and the next moment part of the propeller would become visible as the wave passed by. Flying fish were still to be seen and there seemed to be more birdlife around, albatrosses and other birds. I supposed this was because we were near to land, even though there was none in sight.

We had a group of 'wharfies' onboard on their way to a union conference in the UK. There was much repartee between them and Captain Milne when he was on the bridge and they were playing deck games directly below. Sometimes the Captain got really annoyed at some of the things they said. On one occasion they yelled out: "Can't you make this boat go any faster?" The Captain was completely incensed and shouted back: "How many times do I have to tell you buggers that the *Moreton*

Bay is a *SHIP*, not a *BOAT!*"

I decided to have a bit of fun myself, and see if I could drive a couple of golf balls into the Arabian Sea. I asked one of the stewards if I could get into the baggage room to get my golf clubs. He was incredulous until I told him what I wanted to do. He said he would come and watch me. I got out my driver and set up a couple of balls on makeshift tees on a hatch cover. Under the watchful eyes of the steward, I hit a few balls quite well considering the motion of the ship, but they didn't go far after they encountered the slipstream on the ship's side. But they were *the longest golf balls I had ever hit*, a record in fact, not stopping until they reached the floor of the Arabian Sea, many thousands of feet below! The steward reckoned it was worth seeing and took my driver back to the baggage room.

Life onboard continued on its happy way as we entered the Gulf of Aden. I had discovered the ship's library, so I began to do a bit of reading. I also had my hair cut by the ship's barber, who seemed to do a fair job. There was no need to change our money for use in Aden, as we had changed from Australian to UK money after we left Fremantle. The pound sterling was readily accepted. We were told the *Moreton Bay* would be spending a full day in Aden, arriving late at night and leaving the next evening.

Tuesday 18th December: I woke to find that the *Moreton Bay* was anchored away from the wharves as in Colombo, so I imagined that there was not much freight to be transferred. Any mail and whatever else would be transferred by lighter. Motor launches were provided for us to get ashore to the city of Aden were free.

We went ashore as a group and I found Aden to be a stark, dry, city. Most of the buildings appeared to be made of mud bricks, cream in colour, similar to the roads. To the rear of the city were grey, dry, barren, jagged hills, which I reckoned were about 800 m high. The day, although very hot, was not as humid as in Colombo: In fact, it was quite pleasant, just like a really hot day in Melbourne.

Aden, located in Southern Yemen, had been a Crown colony since 1839. It was an important coaling and oil bunkering station for ships using the Suez Canal. Surprisingly, for such a dry and barren looking land, it was also a good source of fresh water. Not for our ablutions, however, just for the *Moreton Bay*. The Arabs here wore turbans and also a funny-looking hat called a fez.

Some passengers bought them as souvenirs. There were also the usual fabrics and clothing for sale, as well as carvings and trinkets. I wrote a very quick short letter to my family about the voyage to Aden and posted it at the last minute. Back on board, we amused ourselves watching the gully-gully boats before we cast off.

⚓

ADEN TO SUEZ AND BITTER LAKES

Distance: 1,309 Nautical miles. Steaming time: 3 days 15 hours.

The *Moreton Bay* left Aden in the late afternoon and I was on deck to witness the spectacular sight of the rugged mountains behind Aden silhouetted against a hazy blue sky. During the night we turned north to enter

Leaving Aden

38

the Red Sea. The next morning I saw a few small islands off the coast of Eritrea and Ethiopia ('the horn of Africa') in the west. Looking at a map it can be seen why it was given this name because it looked like the horn of a rhinoceros. Yemen was to the east. The Red Sea gradually widened out to around 200 km. The only land to be seen was the occasional tip of a mountain peak in the east.

I asked the Chief Steward if I could go down and see the ship's engines. I was soon being escorted by one of the officers down to the engine room, where it was suffocatingly hot. The *Moreton Bay* was driven by steam turbines which, being enclosed in housings, together with the reduction gearing, were not as interesting to see as a reciprocating engine would have been, with the cranks rotating and the and connecting rods moving rhythmically up and down. I didn't see the boiler room, which must have been as hot as a furnace.

I was, however, very interested to see the large diameter propeller shafts revolving in their bearing blocks. They reminded me of the much smaller propeller shaft of the 75 foot ocean-going tugs I helped build at the Victorian Railways during the war years.

The weather was still very hot as the *Moreton Bay* steamed along the 1.700-km long Red Sea. The water in the pool was so warm that it was no longer refreshing to have a swim. The Red Sea was said to be the warmest in the world, with a very high salt content of about 4%. It was so-called because on occasions it became infested with billions of microscopic red algae, which gave the water a red tinge.

Leaving behind the Red Sea we entered the Gulf of Suez. My little information booklet told me that further up the Gulf was a place called Ras Abu Deraj (meaning "stairs"), which was where the Israelites were supposed to have crossed the Red Sea in Biblical times. In Napoleon's time, it was able to be crossed on horseback. The depth now varies from 75 to 125 m. I was soon able to see the high mountains to the east. Mt Sinai at 2.298 m (7,539 ft) and Jebel Katherina at 2.630 m (8,628 ft), both on the Sinai Peninsula. These mountains were not what I would term beautiful, but looked barren and dry.

Sunday 23rd December: Just before dawn we passed by Suez, and during the day entered the Bitter Lakes where the *Moreton Bay* dropped anchor to wait to be included in a convoy of about twelve ships to enter the canal. We arrived here at a turbulent period in the canal's history when the Egyptians were attempting to take control of the canal from Great Britain. This all began when there was a move to overthrow the so-called 'playboy' King of Egypt, King Farouk.

⚓

BITTER LAKES TO PORT SAID

Distance 163 km total Canal Time taken 12 hours
The total steaming time to pass through the canal
from Suez to Port Said is an average of 17 hours.

Monday 24th December: Christmas Eve. At breakfast, we got a pleasant surprise when we received a four-page card from the Captain inviting us to Christmas dinner the next day.

Soon after breakfast, the *Moreton Bay* raised anchor and entered the Suez Canal in the middle of a convoy to begin its slow transit along the canal to Port Said and the Mediterranean.

The canal was built in the 19th century by Frenchman Ferdinand de Lesseps, to join the Red Sea to the Mediterranean Sea. Construction began in April 1859 and was completed in

40

1869 when the *L'Aigle*, owned by Empress Eugenie of France a cousin of de Lesseps, was the first ship to sail through the canal. At the time when we passed along the Suez Canal, it had a depth of 15 m and a minimum width of 60 m, with both banks lined by rocks.

Nearly all the passengers went up on deck to watch as we steamed along the canal, a unique experience especially as it was Christmas Eve. Surprisingly, there was an extremely cold wind blowing across the desert and the deck of our ship. It was amazing how quickly the temperature dropped after leaving the Red Sea. I was always under the impression that deserts were hot places. Most of us only left the deck to go below for meals.

Steaming along the canal could become boring, but as evidence of the unsettled state between Egypt and Great Britain, every now and again we passed small British army camps beside the canal.

Later we passed some labourers working with pick and shovel, close by on the canal banks. As the *Moreton Bay* passed slowly by, they shouted out: "Sink you dirty fucking British!" These obscenities together with many others were shouted out in perfectly understandable English. All the ladies on deck quickly left and went below. We passed some more shouting obscenities further along the canal, but except for a bit of abuse yelled back at them by some of our wharfies, the rest of us remained silent.

At Port Said our ship passed by the statue of Ferdinand de Lesseps, but we did not stop at Port Said, which looked like a very big city, but entered the Mediterranean Sea on our way to Malta. Steaming through the canal on Christmas Eve 1951 was quite an exciting experience for me, being able to observe the wonderful masterpiece of civil engineering construction, and of course, being abused by the Egyptians.

The sketches are by and of members of our canasta group.

PORT SAID TO MALTA

Distance: 937 Nautical miles. Steaming time: 2 days 14 hours

Tuesday 25th December: Christmas Day. We woke to find that it was a rather cold Christmas Day and we were out of sight of land. We had put up a few Christmas decorations after we left the canal and the lounge bar looked great. We had a few drinks and wished each other a Merry Christmas as we waited excitedly to enter the dining room for Christmas dinner.

While in the Bitter Lakes I had written to the family telling them about Aden and the voyage to the Suez Canal and how I was looking forward to going along the canal. I was expecting to post it in Port Said, but I had to keep it until we got to Malta.

At last, the time came for us to go down to the B deck dining room which was gaily decorated. I sat down at a table with Leon. We shook hands with those around us and wished them a Merry Christmas, some of whom we had never seen before. Soon the stewards came to each table with the entrée and steaming plates of Christmas dinner.

We devoured the entrée, the turkey, and finally the Christmas pudding. A bottle of champagne was provided for each table, so by the time we had finished the dinner, we could hardly move, but found enough energy to go up to the lounge bar to have after-dinner drinks and relax.

Every one of our group signed the Captain's Christmas card, which I still have today. The most vivacious person of our group was Jan, a very talented young lady, who drew most of the sketches of the young people in our group on the cards, which are wonderful momentous of the voyage. Jan was 'the life of the party,' as the saying goes, which of course was our group of canasta players.

As we were enjoying our drinks, we were approached by a couple of the English passengers from across the lounge. They asked us if we would like to join them in serving the crew their Christmas dinner, for which they had already obtained permission from Captain Milne. We thought this was a nice Christmas gesture, so we agreed to take part and were soon given the word to proceed down to the galley adjacent to the crew`s dining room.

Throwing tea towels over our arms to look the part of waiters, we began taking out the plates of Christmas dinners, which were of the same high standard as ours. The crew were all in good spirits, too good, in fact, as it turned out. Serving the Christmas dinner was going really well and I was enjoying the experience. About half of the crew had been served their dinner, when all of a sudden a salt cellar came flying through the air, landing on the plate with Christmas dinner that one of us was carrying and broke it, with the result that the succulent Christmas dinner ended up on the floor!

This was the signal for a fight to start, with plates, cutlery, Christmas dinners and more salt and pepper shakers being thrown. It was mayhem like those comedy shows where you see a plate of cream or such being planted on someone's face, the beginning of food being thrown everywhere. But this wasn't a comedy but a serious fracas.

We felt it was getting a bit dangerous, so we disappeared into the galley, where we helped ourselves to ice cream, and as we did, the joyous cry rang out: "THIS IS REALLY LIVING!" It really was I thought, although a bit dangerous.

The outcome of this unfortunate fracas was that there was no more Christmas dinner for the crew, and some of them were locked up in the brig. It was a great shame. After gorging ourselves on the ice cream, we eventually returned to the lounge bar and back to our canasta and drinking. What was left of Christmas Day passed by pleasantly, in wonderful company.

Wednesday 26th December: Boxing Day was cold and the seas became very rough. I decided to go to the bow and watch as the ship cut through the waves and I enticed Leon to come with me. We made our way around hatches and winches until we reached the 'sharp end' where we could look over the railing. It was very exciting seeing the olive green bow, plough through the waves and we were starting to get very wet from the spray. Suddenly a loud voice boomed at us from the bridge: "You two silly buggers come back from there immediately!" It was Captain Milne shouting at us through a megaphone, so of course, we immediately obeyed his order. On reflection, I must admit it was rather dangerous!

In the evening we amused ourselves with the usual game of canasta, as well as teasing the disgruntled English sitting opposite us in the lounge bar. We were telling them that in a short time they would be back in their beloved England, but before long they would probably want to return to sunny Australia. They now accepted all our jibes in good humour. I think they may have felt a little guilty involving us in the crew's Christmas dinner fiasco.

The swimming pool was no longer filled, as it was too cold. However, I had found another very pleasant form of entertainment, which I was sorry I was not aware of earlier in the voyage. The day before we reached Malta, I wandered into the small theatre where we saw a movie every now and again. I discovered a four-piece ensemble playing classical chamber music. The quartet consisted of a violin, viola, clarinet and flute. I sat down and listened with great joy, especially when I learned that they played there each day at 4 p.m. and for the remainder of the voyage that was where I would be at 4 p.m. It was a pity that there was no mention of them in the information booklet.

Just before we arrived in Malta I wrote a letter to my family telling them how thrilling it was going along the Suez Canal on Christmas Eve, and on Christmas day. It was a delicious Christmas Dinner we were served, but I didn't mention the crew's Christmas Dinner fracas. I wrote how I was thinking of them on Christmas day. *The Moreton Bay* reached the

Malta harbour and Valletta

famous island of Malta, steaming into the Grand Harbour past Mt Sceberras, a rocky promontory at the head of the harbour. We were told our ship would be staying here for a day and a half. The *Moreton Bay* was anchored much closer to the wharves than at Aden and Colombo. Tenders were provided to get to the wharf, or we could hire small rowing boats.

Leon and I caught a tender to the wharf and then a goods lift took us up to street level, where I found a letterbox and posted both letters. From there we made our way to Valletta, the capital and largest town in Malta. The town was very busy, with stone surfaced streets leading here and there. The shops were selling the usual clothing and fabrics, but also glassware, jewellery and a lot of beautiful lace work. We wandered a kilometre or so up a hill behind Valletta.

Malta we discovered was a rather flat island approximately 30 km long and 12 km wide composed of limestone. I read that the island had been called 'the unsinkable aircraft carrier and fortress.' This was because Malta played a key role for the Allies during World War II, as an airbase for planes protecting convoys and raids against the Axis forces, as well as a submarine base and fueling station. The Axis powers tried to render Malta dysfunctional by a prolonged siege, during which the island took a severe battering. In the course of the siege, there were 3,343 air raid alerts, with 16,000 tons of bombs dropped, 2,500 planes were shot down, but Malta was not subdued. After the war, the island was awarded the George Cross, Britain's highest award for civil bravery.

There wasn't much more of interest to see, not even any war damage, but there may have been some on the rest of the Island. We went back to the town centre where we found a narrow, descending stone-paved street, called The Gut, along which all the bars, strip joints, cafes and restaurants were situated. Further along The Gut, there was the red light area, which of course was a popular haunt of the sailors from all the ships that called into Malta. Leon and I sat down at sidewalk cafe, where we had a bite to eat and a beer, and watched the local people of Malta pass by. Many of the ladies were dressed in black.

We joined the group further down The Gut, where I left Leon and the group immersing themselves in the local scene, having a great time drinking cold, Maltese beer and listening to loud, but pleasant music coming from a bar nearby. I wanted to be back on board by 4 p.m. to listen to my newfound music quartet, much better than that in The Gut, in my opinion.

The *Moreton Bay* was scheduled to sail at noon the next day, so only a couple of us went ashore. Leon and I went back to The

Gut and sat at another café, again soaking up the local atmosphere and sipping a nice cold Maltese beer. We returned to the ship to wave goodbye to Malta, which was certainly an island well worth visiting because of its wartime history.

⚓

MALTA TO CEUTA

Distance: 991 Nautical miles. Steaming time: 3 days
Note: Because Ceuta is not listed as a port of call on this voyage
I have calculated the distance and steaming time above from maps.

On the stroke of noon, our ship raised its anchor and began its voyage to Ceuta in Spanish Morocco, opposite the Rock of Gibraltar. The weather was clear, but windy, as we settled down for the penultimate leg of our voyage. I spent the afternoon with the group playing canasta and writing a letter to the family.

I was wakened during the night by the movement of the ship as it rolled and bucked, but eventually went back to sleep.

'In the morning I discovered we were in the middle of a howling gale and rain squalls, with big seas raging all around us. It was a great experience, which I thoroughly enjoyed. When we went down to breakfast, the fiddles had to be fitted, and once again it was great fun controlling our plates and cutlery. I was amazed how well the dining room stewards were able to serve our meals, balancing plates on their hands and arms compensating for the movement of the ship.

I was completely immune to seasickness by now, as most of us were, so we were able to enjoy the pitching and rolling of our ship to the full. The next day the squally weather had not abated, in fact, it was much wilder and rougher, far worse than we had experienced in the Great Australian Bight. The fiddles were fitted to the tables again, and we called out our cry of: "THIS REALLY LIVING!" Once again very appropriate for the conditions.

I was surprised that seas of this size could be generated in the Mediterranean, which was bordered by land on each side. I did not imagine that there was enough 'reach' (a clear uninterrupted stretch of water) to allow such large waves to be generated as we were experiencing. The Great Australian Bight has a reach that extends all the way from the Antarctic and Africa, but I supposed that as we were steaming directly into the teeth of a westerly gale, there was the full length of the Mediterranean to enable large waves to be generated. The Captain told us that he was slowing down the *Moreton Bay* to enable the ship to ride the waves better.

The following morning the wind had dropped and the waves were not as high. It had been very exciting watching our ship battle the wild seas as the waves broke over her bow in clouds of spray, nevertheless, it was a great relief that this was behind us and we were in calmer waters. Land was now beginning to close in on us from both sides: Spain on the right (starboard) and Morocco on the left (port). The coastlines we could see on each side of our ship would nearly join together soon to form the Strait of Gibraltar.

The weather had cleared, so I went up on deck, where I was delighted to see the tops of snow-covered mountains to our right. I looked at a map in the ship's library and found that they were the mountains of the Sierra Nevada in Spain near Granada that rose to heights of over 3.000 m (9,000 ft). I was thrilled to see the snow because in a month or two I hoped to be skiing in Austria or Switzerland, or maybe both.

As our ship approached Ceuta, Gibraltar 425 m (1,394 ft)

high poked its head above the horizon, Captain Milne announced over the PA. His message was: "In a short time we will be arriving at Ceuta in Spanish Morocco. It will be New Year's Eve and celebrations will be in full sway in the city. You will be permitted to go ashore, but the *Moreton Bay* will be leaving Ceuta promptly at 10 p.m. so make sure you are all aboard."

Monday 31st December: Just before noon on New Year's Eve 1951, the *Moreton Bay* backed into the wharf, hitting it with a solid bump, literally our first contact with the city of Ceuta in Spanish Morocco!

The port of Ceuta is located directly opposite the Rock of Gibraltar across the 16 km wide Strait of Gibraltar, which is the only connection the Mediterranean has to the Atlantic Ocean. It was wonderful to be able to gaze on the famous landmark of Gibraltar guarding the entrance to the Mediterranean. I knew about Gibraltar from the war years, and the value Great Britain placed on this territory. It was said of Gibraltar that it was 'the rock upon which the Axis hopes in the Mediterranean foundered.' Such was its importance during the last war.

Leon and I and a couple of our group got together and quickly went ashore to see the city, from which we could hear the noise of New Year's Eve celebrations. We found men and women in gaily coloured clothes, shawls and hats, dancing in the streets to music that was broadcast all around the city by banks of loudspeakers attached to nearly every light pole. There was much to buy at the various shops, mostly beautiful, Spanish style laces, hats, beads, and scarves. Many of the wares related to Spanish bullfighting.

One very popular item was wine and liqueurs in bottles shaped like a Spanish bullfighter. One of these was anisette, a clear liquid, which I supposed was derived from a form of aniseed. It looked rather potent. I didn't buy anything except a colourful silk scarf, as I had already spent more than I had planned during the voyage.

As it grew dark the city lit up with beautiful multi-coloured lights. Hit tunes of the day were being broadcast from the loudspeakers and many of the people were singing joyfully as they mingled together. One was a rhythmic samba called 'Canto la Gusto,' sung by Carmen Miranda, a singer that I greatly admired. She was born in Portugal, but went to Brazil where she made a career for herself as a singer, dancer and film star, becoming known as the 'Brazilian Bombshell.' She was famous for her 15 cm high stiletto shoe heels, bare midriffs and colourful skirts, but most of all for the huge headgear she wore, which was adorned with fruit.

We had a great time in the city where a couple of times we couldn't help but yell out our cry. "THIS IS REALLY LIVING!" We truly were really living on an absolutely fabulous voyage. Being in Ceuta on New Year's Eve, there could not have been a more joyful place to spend the last day of 1951, than in this foreign port on the other side of our world, where the joy of living was in abundance. Reluctantly we made our way back to the ship for our 10 p.m. departure

Whether Captain Milne had any control over our 10 p.m. departure time or not, I wasn't sure, but I tended to think he did, because it ensured that all his passengers would be safely onboard and not become involved in the celebrations ashore at midnight. I also wondered if he had any hand in bringing the *Moreton Bay* to Ceuta just at the right time to allow his passengers to enjoy a colourful, musical and happy New Year's Eve in Spanish Morocco. I never found the answer to this question or why Ceuta was not mentioned in the information book. I have come to the conclusion however unlikely that our very popular Captain Milne planned it all himself.

⚓

CEUTA to SOUTHAMPTON
Distance: 1.325 Nautical miles. Steaming time: 4 days

Just on 10 p.m. the *Moreton Bay* pulled away from the wharf. We could still hear the music as we watched the coloured lights until they faded into the night, wishing that we would have liked to have been in the city to see in the New Year.

Just after the ship left Ceuta I saw Kay, one of the New Zealand girls, stagger through the doorway on to the dimly lit deck. I followed her to make sure she was all right. She sat down on the deck with her back to the cabins, so I joined her. She had definitely had too much to drink, probably Anisette, I thought. We sat and talked for quite a while until the Master at Arms came by and accused me of molesting her. "I certainly was not!" I replied angrily, and Kay said tersely, "He was doing no such thing, so go away and leave us alone!"

The Master at Arms was taken aback by Kay's abrupt reply, but demonstrated the power of his rank, saying gruffly: "Both of you get up, leave the deck and go inside immediately!" That was an order, so I escorted Kay back into the lounge bar where we told the others what had happened. They thought it was a huge joke, exclaiming together: "THIS IS REALLY LIVING." Under my breath I said to myself sarcastically, 'a bloke tries to do a good deed for the last time in the year, and what happens? Unbelievable!'

By means of a very nice colourful card delivered to each of us, Captain Milne invited us to a Landfall Dinner on 1st January.

See below. We thought this would be a wonderful dinner for which we would dress in our best, and of course, I would bring out my dinner suit. When I unpacked the case and took out my dinner suit I thought I would never be able to get the creases out of it. I tried with one of the ship's irons but gave up as I thought I might scorch it.

Tuesday 1st January 1952: **New Year's Day.** We watched our watches, which we continually had to adjust as we passed into new time zones and at last we heard the eagerly awaited ship's watch bell ring out indicating it was midnight! We all yelled, screamed, hugged and kissed each other. We shook hands with the English in the bar opposite. I was sure we were all like me, wondering what adventures and experiences 1952 would bring to our lives. I shook hands with Leon and thanked him for inviting me to go abroad with him.

Soon after leaving Ceuta the *Moreton Bay* entered the Atlantic Ocean and we began to encounter large swells as we headed towards Southampton. I had recovered from my hangover, and in the afternoon I listened with joy to the musical ensemble that exhibited no signs of any musical hangover. From day to day the ensemble changed the instruments. It was always a pleasantly relaxing half hour before I had my couple of beers, but tonight's dinner was very special. I wished the members of the ensemble a Happy New Year and thanked them for the pleasure they had given me with their music.

I dressed in my dinner suit for the Captain's dinner and at the appointed time went down to the dining room together with

<table>
<tr><td>

t.s.s Moreton Bay

———

CAPTAIN N. S. MILNE

———

In the old circle, day by day,
  The sea-line cuts the Sky ;
Night after night upon their way
  The ancient stars go by.

No change there seems, but as we move
  The sea has lost its name
And found another ; and above
  The stars are not the same.

J. W. Mackail.

———

Tuesday, 1st January, 1952

</td><td>

Landfall   Dinner

———

CREAM MACDONALD

FRIED FILLET of HALIBUT, TOMATO SAUCE

RICE POLONAISE

SAVOURY LAMB'S HEARTS

ROAST NORFOLK TURKEY, ST. JAMES

CUMBERLAND HAM

BROWNED and BOILED POTATOES

FRESH GARDEN PEAS

OLD ENGLISH PLUM PUDDING, SWEET SAUCE

FRUIT SALAD

ICE CREAM

DESSERT   COFFEE

</td></tr>
</table>

Leon and some others in our group. Everybody had dressed up in their best clothes and all the ladies looked very attractive. I hadn't managed to get all the creases out of my dinner suit, but I received some comments that I was very clever to have included the suit in my luggage. I thought I was too! There were murmurs of anticipation and lots of animated talk around the tables, but very quickly this ceased as the waiters began bringing out the dinners. The *Moreton Bay* was rolling languidly during the dinner, but not enough to require the fiddles to be fitted.

The dinner was excellent, as were all the meals during the voyage. Everyone at our table and members of our canasta group signed each other's menus. On the slim chance that someone reading this narrative will recognise their names below. Most knew I was a skier, hence some of the comments on the card shown on the previous page.

Best Wishes, Dolly Harris, ---Kaye Jones---- Best of luck Gordon, Jan Moorhead --- X Joan and Elaine Hoban, ---- Happy skids and skis Donald Fish, ---- A good New Year, Peter Bogie All the luck in the world from, Nan Smith, Jocelyn Brown, Pamela Fry---- Mandy Wish and David Wish Till we meet again in Switzerland, Grant Robert, Bob Foster, San Antonio, Texas--- It's been fun knowing you, the best of luck, Josh Just, N.Y. U.S.A.

As I write; I felt that in retrospect there was only one thing missing from the occasion. I thought someone should have stood up and made a speech about the voyage. No one did, but I am going to make a speech in this book to rectify that omission, nearly seventy years after the event. The Captain I noticed, was seated at one of the tables.

I rose from my seat and raising my voice said: "I would like to say a few words." Quietness reigned while I made the following speech.

"First of all, I would like to thank Captain Milne for a safe and carefree voyage, which I am sure will be so all the way to

Southampton. Captain Milne has not only been an excellent Captain of his good ship the *TSS Moreton Bay,* but also a very good host, welcoming us to his dinner table and arranging events for special occasions such as this dinner, together with many other activities that have enhanced our enjoyment of the voyage, which for me has been absolutely fabulous. I am sure many of your passengers will agree with me." This produced a round of here-heres and clapping. "I would now like you to rise and join me in a toast: To Captain Milne, his officers and staff." Everyone raised their glasses clinked them and clapped loudly.

I sat down and, as everyone began to leave the dining room Captain Milne, after shaking hands with a few passengers, approached me, shook my hand and thanked me for the toast.

Wednesday 2nd January 1952: I was recovering from a mild hangover. Remembering that I had been given a small diary, I decided that I would enter the events of each day until I returned to Australia. Amazingly, I managed to do just that every day without fail and the entries on these pages are the basis for this book.

The *Moreton Bay* began crossing the Bay of Biscay and passing Cape Finisterre which is the most westerly point of Spain. The ocean became rough as we entered the English Channel and steamed towards Southampton. Although I was not feeling exactly a 100%, I commenced packing, but soon found that it was too rocky in the cabin. I don't think I was really seasick, even though the ship was rolling quite heavily in the long swells. I think it was more like 'food and drink sick,' as the last few days had been a bit of an assault on my stomach.

Thursday 3rd January 1952: After nearly being thrown out of our bunks during the night, the high seas did not ease until about noon the next day when I felt much better and spent a lot of time in the morning on deck, fascinated by the large swells. This was our last full day aboard, so in the afternoon I spent some time packing and doodling around. I gave tips to our cabin and table steward, £1 each. We all congregated from time to time in the lounge bar, but the canasta had been abandoned and to a large extent so had the drinking. Soon, we would be steaming in English waters and tax would have to be added to anything we bought. Knowing this I had previously stocked up on cigarettes.

I asked Leon to tell me about his relationship to Mr. and Mrs. Baker, who were going to put us up until we left on our backpacking tour on the Continent. Leon told me their son Howard had immigrated to Melbourne, where he met and married Leon's sister. That was a great surprise to me, as I had heard Howard Baker many times in Melbourne, reading the news on 3AR and 3LO.

As the *Moreton Bay* was passing through this very rough stretch of sea, we heard on the wireless that a maritime epic was being played out further to the west. Off the southern coast of England, a small freighter, the *Flying Enterprise*, captained by a Dane, Captain Carlson, sustained damage in the high seas and began to sink.

Friday 4th January 1952: The *Moreton Bay* arrived in Southampton at 9 a.m. After a welter of hugs and handshaking all-round, Leon and I disembarked. Walking down the gangway of the *Moreton Bay* at Southampton brought to a conclusion a fabulous voyage; one of the most enjoyable, and certainly the most relaxing and interesting, five weeks of my life. Sailing to England on a one-class, medium-sized ship was a true voyage of discovery.

The trouble that appeared to involve the purser while the

Moreton Bay was in Fremantle, and the fracas at the crew's Christmas dinner, did not in any way lessen my opinion that the voyage was absolutely fabulous in every respect. In fact, they added an element of drama to the experience.

I took one last look back at our wonderful ship the *TSS Moreton Bay* and began the next stage of my grand adventure. Sadly for the present-day tourist and backpacker, this mode of travel is no longer possible.

*A last look at our wonderful rugged
ship the TSS Moreton Bay*

CHAPTER FIVE
IN ENGLAND AFTER THE VOYAGE

Our first step on English soil was on the wharf and on the platform of the Southampton railway station, where we climbed aboard a train for London. Our luggage had already been put on the train to be collected when we arrived in London. It was a great thrill for me to see my first English locomotive a School's Class, which had been an object of my childhood admiration. Leon and I didn't see much of the English countryside on the way to London, as the train windows were fogged up and it was quite misty outside. When we got off the train at Waterloo Station, all the luggage was brought to a central point on the station for us to identify and collect.

There to welcome us was Netta Higgins, an attractive young lady that Leon and I had skied with in the YHA. It was a wonderful surprise, and a little puzzling, because we didn't know that Netta was in London. She told us that one of her YHA friends had written to her about our voyage. After we had recovered from that unexpected and joyful welcome, we made a note of Netta's address and telephone number and waved her goodbye.

We gathered up all our luggage (or so I thought) and hired a taxi to take us across London from Waterloo Station at to King's Cross Station, which was on the opposite side of the city. On the way across London in the taxi, the only London landmarks we recognised were the Thames River, which we crossed over on Waterloo Bridge, very exciting, because I remembered seeing the movie *Waterloo Bridge* some years earlier.

Arriving safely at King's Cross Station, with its large imposing entrance and central clock tower, we caught a steam hauled train to Hitchin in Hertfordshire. The journey took about 30 minutes, but once again we didn't see much from the windows because of a heavy mist. We climbed out of the train at Hitchin with our luggage and took a taxi through the mist and cold to Mr. and Mrs. Baker's house, which was not very far from the station, arriving there about noon. Mr. and Mrs. Baker, a lovely middle-aged couple immediately made us very welcome.

After we commenced unpacking, I suddenly realised I had not collected my rucksack with the rest of my luggage at Waterloo Station. *I had lost my rucksack!* I suppose it was the excitement of arriving in London, together with the surprise of seeing Netta. Leon said he didn't remember seeing my rucksack there. I was devastated. My Andy Broad framed rucksack contained all my skiing clothes, sleeping bag, hike tent, golf shoes and jacket, as well as many other items of clothing and skiing gear. We wondered if my rucksack had actually been taken from the train, or indeed if it had been taken off the *Moreton Bay.*

During the two weeks before crossing the Channel to begin our backpacking tour in Austria, we explored London. I had an exciting meeting with my girlfriend Judy and I took her to a show. However, our romance was off as we decided to enjoy our time abroad.

Nearly every day I rang London Transport, Southampton Wharf Authority, Waterloo Station, British Rail and other lost property places that I thought might have knowledge of my rucksack, but with no success.

The week before we were due to leave England, I came to the conclusion that my rucksack was gone for good. I bought new equipment, but only those items that were essential for the backpacking tour we were about to begin. Rucksack, sleeping bag and skiing clothes.

Two days prior to leaving on the tour, I had just come back to the Bakers from shopping in Hitchin. When the door opened I saw that everyone had a big smile on their faces. They led me into the lounge room where, surprise, surprise, on the floor was my rucksack! There was also a letter from my mother, but I left that unread until I checked the contents of my rucksack and found everything was all there. Joy-Oh-Joy! My mother's letter was full of news. How the family missed me and how they had received all the letters I had sent from the voyage.

The way my rucksack came to be delivered to the Bakers was a bit of a mystery, Mr. and Mrs. Baker seemed to think a railway official brought it. I never did find out the story of where it had been. There were no tags on it, which might have given us a clue as to its whereabouts since it arrived at Southampton. I went to sleep that night very relieved, feeling like a millionaire.

During the week there were a lot of articles about the *Flying Enterprise* in newspapers that we had heard was in trouble as we steamed towards Southampton. It was an epic of maritime history. We learned that the crew were taken off by helicopter, but Captain Carlson refused to leave. Dancy, a man from a tug standing by went aboard, and with help from Captain Carlson secured a tow line to the stricken vessel, but this broke some days later. Even though the ship had a 45-degree list, Captain Carlson still refused to leave. However, when the ship's list increased to the horizontal, the two brave men Captain Carlson and Dancy, walked along the funnel into the cold sea, where they were rescued. The ship finally sank on 10th January 1952.

The last moments of the Flying Enterprise

CHAPTER SIX

MY EXCITING LIFE BETWEEN VOYAGES

Thursday 24th January 1952: Leon and I crossed the English Channel and travelled by train through Strasbourg, Basle, Innsbruck, Salzburg and finally to Bad Ischl, where four days later, without prior warning, Leon left me. Believe or not, the same day Leon left me I was invited to stay with and an Austrian family.

Very soon after Leon left me, I was invited to stay with an Austrian family in Bad Ischl. During my stay with them, on the radio after dinner on 6th February, we heard the unexpected and sad news of the death of King George VI in Sandringham. Princess Elizabeth was holidaying in Kenya when she heard the news of her father's death. I found that I was touched deeply by the King's death.

I quickly realised how fortuitous it was for me that the death of King George V1 occurred during this year of my time abroad. I was sure that next year, 1953 in the spring, our new Queen, Queen Elizabeth II would be crowned, so I would definitely plan to be in London for that marvellous, once in a lifetime occasion.

I spent ten days with the Austrian family who had looked after very well and then I continued on through occupied Austria by myself discovering that touring alone is the best way to travel, no need for any compromise on the how, where and when and I toured.

After leaving Austria I visited Italy and Switzerland, where I skied for three weeks the last two of which were with Netta, who had welcomed Leon and me on Waterloo Station. I returned to England on 29th March 1952 after my two-month-long, spectacular tour.

I found a job in my trade, in Stevenage England. One day I went to London and visited Australia House as most Aussies do, where amongst other very useful information posted on notice boards; the Orient Line had a notice requesting Australians to register with the company for passages to Australia.

Although I had no intention of returning home until after the Coronation, I decided to register my name. I went to the Orient Line offices, where one of the brochures that I was given showed the ports that Orient Line ships called into, one of which was Naples. Immediately I had a brilliant idea. I would join the ship in Naples after I had toured down through France and Italy. With a sense of relief, I booked a passage back to Australia from Naples sometime in October 1953 and paid a deposit of £10. The Orient Line said that they would let me know the exact date of sailing, and the ship I would be sailing on. The die was cast!

I worked for three months in Stevenage and on 3rd August 1952, I began my second two-month-long backpacking tour. As it was on my first tour, virtually all my accommodation was in Youth Hostels (YH). I backpacked through Scotland, Norway, Sweden, Denmark, Austria and returned to England through the Netherlands on the 30th October 1952, after another long, enthralling tour.

I worked in London at my trade for eleven months living as a Londoner. In early December 1952, I received a message from the Orient Line office informing me that I had secured a passage on the P and O ship *Orion*, sailing on Friday 18th September 1953 from Naples. It was scheduled to reach Port Melbourne on 13th October 1953, my mother's birthday. Wonderful I thought, it would be a really beaut birthday present for her.

While still working in London and enjoying immensely my busy social life as a Londoner, in July 1953, I received a message from the Orient Line to come into the office and pay the balance of the voyage money. I went straight in and paid the balance of my voyage ticket (£30/15) and confirmed that the sailing date from Naples was still Friday 18th September.

The total cost of the voyage was £80/15. They gave me my dining table number and I arranged for a carrier to come on Wednesday 19th August 1953 to pick up my luggage to put on the ship. I asked if there were any information pamphlets about the *Orion* and the voyage. There wasn't. The agent said all I would need to know about the voyage would be posted on the notice boards on the ship. That was a bit troubling compared to very informative booklets I was given before the voyage on the *Moreton Bay* by the Aberdeen and Commonwealth Line agents.

The carrier came and took my luggage, two cases, golf clubs and skis, and now I was just waiting for next Thursday to begin my journey back to Australia.

CHAPTER SEVEN

MY JOURNEY BACK HOME BEGINS

Thursday 20th August 1953: I waved goodbye to London, and began my third and last backpacking tour. This tour, however, had one component that the other two lacked. *Every step I took brought me closer to home.* I crossed the English Channel and staying in Youth Hostels (YH). I hitchhiked and backpacked my way through Paris, Lyon, Grenoble and on to the French Riviera at Cannes and Nice.

I had a wonderful time in Cannes and Nice the so-called 'playground of the rich and famous.' In Nice, I bought a rail ticket to Naples, because I wasn't sure that hitchhiking in southern Italy would be as easy as it was in France. I had to be sure to be Naples in time to board the *Orion* on Friday 18th September.

The ticket allowed me to stop off wherever I wished on the way. I visited Monaco, San Remo, La Spezia, Pisa and Rome, finally reaching Naples in the late afternoon of Sunday 12th September.

This left me with five days to explore the surrounding country before boarding the *Orion*. The five days were full of interest. I explored Naples, visited Pompeii, and spent three days on the beautiful Isle of Capri. I stayed in the YH in Naples, which was on the top floor of the Grille Hotel.

CHAPTER EIGHT
SOME TRICKERY BOARDING THE ORION

Friday 18th September: I rose very early and saw the *Orion* enter the harbour at 7 a.m. The *Orion, at first sight,* looked a larger and more modern ship than the *Moreton Bay.* The hull was painted a yellowish colour with white decks which made it look quite elegant. A young Australian lady approached me at breakfast in the YH and asked me if I could help her to get on board the *Orion?* She was the same lady I had seen yesterday, trying to entice two Americans to help her stow away. She said her name was Dot and told me that she had been to the Orient Line office in Naples to try and get a passage.

Dot told me the Italian shipping officer said there were no vacancies, but if she would sleep with him, he would get her a ticket. She would not agree to his proposition, but from this encounter, she knew there must be a berth available. Dot. I thought, was just short of 30 years old, a blonde, but not really attractive to me, quite plain in fact with a slight hare lip.

Dot went on to tell me that she had just come from a Communist convention in Russia and it was essential that she got a passage on the *Orion*. She said she had a plan to get aboard and asked me again if I would help her? I was a little cautious but listened to what she had to say.

Her plan seemed to be fairly simple, and would not involve me in any act that would cause me trouble, so I agreed to do as she wished. I was not aware that this good deed would not only cause me considerable annoyance, but would prevent me from having a relaxing time for most of the voyage back to Australia. A troubling voyage in fact. I suppose I should have been wary of doing good turns for people connected with ships, because the two good turns I was involved in on the *Moreton Bay,* the Christmas dinner and Kay after visiting Ceuta on New Year's Eve, backfired.

Dot took me aside and said: "Here is my plan. I will hire a horse-drawn buggy, and we will both go in style right up to the gates of the wharf. We will get off the buggy, and I want you to have your ticket and passport ready, and slowly walk to the gates. I will be close behind you. I want you to keep your rucksack pushed to one side, to leave room for me to get past you." I listened to her plan and after I got her to explain it a bit more I said: "OK I will do my best."

Immediately after breakfast, we booked out of the YH together and Dot hired a horse-drawn buggy from a stand close by. Off we went in style as planned to the wharf, where Dot asked the buggy driver to pull up close to the gates to let us off. This I imagined was to make a good impression with the gatekeepers. We alighted together from the buggy and Dot paid the fare.

I waited for Dot and then walked just ahead of her to the

boarding gate. While the
customs officer was checking
my ticket and passport, Dot
pushed past me and ran like hell
along the wharf with another
officer madly chasing her! I
watched in amazement as Dot
reached the gangway first, ran

The *Orion* tied up in Naples

up it and disappeared, with the customs official not far behind in
hot pursuit.

Dot told me afterwards that she quickly found the purser's
office, showed her passport to the customs officer, purchased a
ticket, and all was well. She only had a small bag with her at the
time and I never knew where the rest of her luggage was, if she
had any.

While all of this was happening I had passed through the
customs and boarding gate OK and was walking slowly along
the wharf, half expecting to be brought to a halt and detained as
her accomplice. This didn't happen, so up the gangplank I went
and I was safely aboard the *Orion*.

At the purser's office, I was welcomed onboard and given my cabin and bunk number. I asked the purser if he had any printed matter to explain about the ship and the voyage. He said that the *Orion* would be raising anchor at 5 p.m. and any other information I required was on the ship's noticeboards. Dot meanwhile was nowhere to be seen. Leaving my rucksack on my bunk, I went back into Naples and shopped for odds and ends, to get rid of all the Italian money I had left.

A Naples shopping arcade

I returned to the ship in time for lunch and was directed to a table where there were some young people about my age. After the introductions, I settled down to enjoy an excellent cold lunch, so different from my usual ham rolls and sandwiches. After lunch, I had a swim in the ship's pool, which was in the stern.

As I wandered around the deck I soon found that this ship was totally different to the *Moreton Bay* because I could not get past gates that were shut, which led to an upper deck in the forward part of the *Orion*. I thought it was about time I had a look at the notice board and see what I could learn about this ship that was about to take me back home.

I discovered that the *Orion* was a two-class ship, first and tourist class. The notice board listed the ports of call and dates of arrival at exactly the same ports of call as the *Moreton Bay*. I was glad to see that October 13th was still the arrival date at Port Melbourne. There was also a warning to passengers that the *Orion* is a mail ship and only remains in ports of call for one day to transfer mail and passengers and leaves promptly on the designated time. I suppose I should have known all about that when I first booked my passage, but not having been given any information about the ship from the P&O agent in London as I had received about the *Moreton Bay* in Melbourne, was a bit troubling.

There were a couple of notice boards and from one, I learned about the *Orion* was built by Vickers-Armstrong in Barrow, England, and was launched in 1934 by the Duke of Gloucester from Australia, via a remote control wireless signal. The *Orion* was driven by geared turbines through twin screws, weighed 24,000 tonnes and has a speed of 20 knots. The *Orion* has accommodation for 546 first-class and 706 tourist class passengers. She was a troop ship in the war beside her sister ship the *Orcades,* which was torpedoed and sunk in 1942. Although the notice boards listed the dates at each port it did not list distances between each port, but the distances are exactly the same as that shown on the *Moreton Bay's* booklet The *Orion* was a larger ship than the *Moreton* bay and faster too.

Not included of course on these notice boards, was that in October 1963, the *Orion* was handed over to the ship breakers in Antwerp Belgium, where it was broken up for scrap.

CHAPTER NINE
A TROUBLING VOYAGE BEGINS

NAPLES TO PORT SAID
Distance: 1.325 Nautical miles. Steaming time: 4 days

At exactly 5 p.m. the *Orion* pulled up anchor and cast off. I was off back to Australia but in a totally different type of ship in which I had such an fabulous voyage from port Melbourne to Southampton. I was rather sad and troubled that I would not be able to walk around the *Orion* from stem to stern, but am relegated to the tourist class stern of the ship.

As the *Orion* steamed out into the bay of Naples, I took one last look at Naples and Vesuvius. I noticed too that Mt Solaro on the Isle of Capri

The author on board the Orion with Vesuvius behind

had again generated an impressive cumulus cloud, very like the day before when I returned on the ferry back to Naples from the island.

I went down to the dining room for very tasty dinner and found that the dining room was air-conditioned, a very welcome asset especially when we sail further south. Welcome too was freshwater for washing and showering, much more refreshing than saltwater we had on the *Moreton Bay*.

I watched the sun dropping behind the cloud over Capri in a blaze of glorious red and orange, my last continental sunset. Then spent the next few hours lounging in the bar over a beer and talking to a few passengers before I retired to my cabin for a well-earned sleep. My cabin mates were two New Zealanders and there was one spare bunk, which we used to store our everyday needs. I dropped off to sleep quickly, but considering the drama of boarding the *Orion* with Dot, not surprisingly I had a nightmare.

Saturday 19th September: It was a beautiful morning out in the middle of the Mediterranean, which was as calm as a millpond. I had a beaut breakfast and salad lunch and then played deck games. Cigarettes and beer were now custom free and cheap

After dinner, there was a dance on the ship's small dance floor, where I talked and danced a little with Dot. She thanked me for my help and I bought her a beer and offered her a cigarette. Later we went up on deck to watch the sea go by. It was a brilliant warm, moonlit night and Dot began waffling on about sex, which embarrassed me. I didn't like it and wondered if she was trying to proposition me. I impulsively gave her a big hard kiss to shut her up, wished her good night and returned to the bar. I had a beer before returning my cabin, where I got a feeling of claustrophobia. However, I climbed into my bunk and had a good night's sleep.

Sunday 20th September: I played a few deck games during

the day. Dot sought me out and I bought her a beer and offered her a cigarette. In the evening we passed Crete, about 60 km away on the port side of the *Orion,* its mountains just visible over the horizon.

Later that night while I was in the lounge bar relaxing, Dot attached herself to me again. I bought myself a beer and smoked a cigarette, but I didn't offer either to her, because I didn't really enjoy her company. Thankfully seeing I wasn't responding to her, Dot left me. I had another beer and chatted to a young German couple. We had an interesting talk together especially about my backpacking tour through Germany.

The ambience in the tourist class bar of the *Moreton Bay* was much different to that on the *Orion,* where there was not much fun or laughter coming from the persons drinking and playing cards and other games.

Monday 21st September. I decided that I would have to shake myself free of Dot, who seemed to expect that I was going to supply her with cigarettes and beer on the voyage. She might be a Communist, and I have nothing really against Communists, but the *Orion* was not a commune. So I tried to ignore her, but as soon as I entered the lounge and bought myself a beer she came and sat beside me, saying: "I know you are trying to avoid me, but the ship is not big enough." After that remark, I got up and found another seat.

Passing the de Lesseps statue at Port Said

About 4 p.m. the *Orion* arrived in Port Said, the northern port of the Suez Canal, named after Egypt's Viceroy at the time of construction of the canal.

The *Orion* passed by the large statue of Ferdinand de Lesseps, the man responsible for the building of the canal.

In 1952 a revolution took place that resulted in King Farouk being overthrown. Colonel Abdel Nasser became President of Egypt in 1954, and in 1956 he seized control of the canal, asserting Egypt's authority over it. The de Lesseps statue was removed during the conflict. Nasser used the tolls to help with another great engineering project, the construction of the Aswan High Dam. The British troops left Egypt, but a short while afterwards, Britain and France attacked Egypt, resulting in the canal being blocked with sunken ships until it was finally cleared in 1975.

When the *Orion* tied up to the wharf in Port Said, and we went down to dinner, we were told over the ship's loudspeakers that we could leave the ship and go into Port Said, a duty-free city. We were warned that on no account were we to go outside the city limits, or to go alone, especially now that darkness had fallen.

Dot asked me if I would take her into Port Said. She said she wanted to buy some things. "Yes, I will take you." I agreed to take her because she couldn't go on her own, and I was sure no one else would have offered.

We walked together down the long sloping gangplank, shared by both tourist and first-class passengers. The gangplank was lined with smart-looking Egyptian soldiers wearing fez hats, all carrying rifles. As we walked down the gangplank, just to our rear, there were several English first-class lady passengers, escorted by some of the ship's officers. One of the ladies said in a loud voice: "What a cheek to have those Egyptian soldiers there." One of the officers quickly turned around to face her and said to her curtly: "Madam, they are there for *your* protection!"

I took Dot into Port Said and stood around bored, while she tried her non-existent feminine charms, bargaining with the Arabs for trinkets and the like. I didn't see anything I wanted to buy. After we returned to the ship, she thanked me, and I said goodnight and left her. I watched the gully gulley boats for a while. I really missed the good times I had in the lounge bar of the *Moreton Bay*, drinking, playing canasta, and generally having a happy time with our young group.

I decided that I must really begin to make friends with some of the young blokes and girls that I saw in the lounge bar and played deck games with, but I got the feeling that they were avoiding me because they thought that Dot was my girlfriend.

PORT SAID TO SUEZ

Note: The total steaming time to pass through the canal from Port Said to Suez is an average of 17 hours.

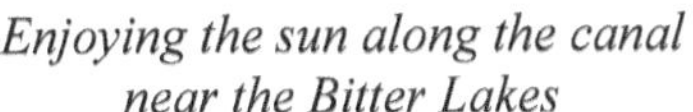

Enjoying the sun along the canal near the Bitter Lakes *Looking back along the canal soon after leaving Port Said*

Tuesday 22nd September: I woke in the morning to find that the *Orion* was halfway along the canal. I relaxed most of the time sitting out on the deck watching the flat and sparsely timbered sides of the canal pass slowly by. The weather was overcast and very hot, the direct opposite of the very cold conditions I had encountered on my way to the UK. This time all the way along the canal from Port Said to the Bitter Lakes no Arabs yelled obscenities at us, although they probably had more reason to this time.

Dot came and plonked herself down on a chair beside me. I thought that if just for once when she sought me out, if she had offered to buy me a beer or offered me a cigarette, I may have looked more kindly at her, but it didn't happen. We didn't have much to say to each other so I decided to go into the bar. Thankfully Dot didn't follow me.

Around lunchtime, the *Orion* dropped its anchor in the Bitter Lakes located about two-thirds of the way along the canal from Port Said. The Bitter Lakes provide a passing and marshalling area for ships travelling in both directions along the canal. I wasn't aware of the *Orion* being arranged for the single file journey along the canal in Port Said, but here we had to wait for the convoy to be arranged.

It wasn't a long wait. After dinner just as it was getting dark the *Orion* pulled up its anchor and steamed out of the Bitter Lakes, joining the convoy to move slowly along the canal toward Suez.

The *Orion* did not have a small classical music ensemble, like I belatedly discovered on the *Moreton Bay,* but I imagined there would have been one in first class. After dinner, I went to the ship's theatre where I saw the movie *Genevieve,* with the theme music played by Larry Adler on his harmonica. The stars of the movie were Kenneth More and Kay Kendall. The story was all about a veteran car race. It was a very funny movie, once again only released that year. It was beginning to get really hot.

SUEZ TO ADEN

Distance: 1,309 Nautical miles. Steaming time: 3 days

Wednesday 23rd September: The *Orion* was now in the middle of the Red Sea and it was very, very hot. I tried to keep out of Dot's way, but it wasn't easy. There was a dance on board and it was quite enjoyable because I was, at last, getting to know a few young people, who had avoided me

A couple of assisted migrants of about my age were seated at our dining table, together with a couple of Aussie blokes and Kiwi girls. The migrants were very quiet. One came from Bristol and the other from near Birmingham. Both were going to Sydney where they had distant relations who were going to look after them. They kept to themselves and were rarely seen in the lounge bar, I suspect because they did not have much spare cash.

I tried to imagine how I would have felt in their place. I was sure it was nothing like the gleeful and pleasant apprehension we Australians felt on our way to the UK. I wrote letters to the family to post in Aden. I thought the letter to my family might accompany me on the *Orion* to Australia.

Thursday 24th September: It was hellish hot. I spent the day having a beer, reading and swimming in the pool in 30°C water,

The Stein from the dance hall in Berchtegaden.

pumped up from the Red Sea, too hot really to be refreshing. In the evening a beer garden was set up by the crew on the rear deck, and a race meeting was organised, complete with betting. Fictitious horse's names were picked out of a small barrel. It was great fun and I was having an exciting time in the mock beer garden, although not one of my horses won or even got a place. Some passengers were also dancing to piped music at the rear of the beer garden.

It was a beautiful night and I was talking again with Gerhart and Edna, a young German couple that I had talked with earlier in the voyage. I was keeping Dot at arm's length.

I decided to go and get my German beer mugs, not only to drink from, but to show Gerhart and Edna. They thought they were great souvenirs, more so when I related how and where I had acquired, or rather stolen them. The small one I pinched from a dance hall in Berchtesgaden, and the other from the Hofbrauhaus in Munich. I have no guilty conscience as I regarded them as war reparations to Australia. I had just filled both beer steins and was drinking from the large stein while I sat on a deck chair and talked.

The stein from the Hofbrauhouse in Munich

Dot, who was rather inebriated, came over and asked me to have a dance with her, or more likely, I imagined, buy her a beer and offer her a cigarette. I said to her:

"Go and find someone else to dance with," then I ignored her and turned away. All of a sudden Dot kicked the leg away from my deckchair, which left me flat on my back! She then picked up both beer mugs that were nearly full and poured the contents all over me as I lay there. Then she tried to tear my shirt off me!

I was lucky I didn't get hurt, but more to the point. If she had damaged the steins or thrown them overboard, I think I would have murdered her. I had heard of the saying: 'Hell has no fury like a woman scorned,' but never for one moment did I think I would experience that fury first hand! 'This is really living.' I thought.

That was definitely the end of Dot for me. No more free cigarettes or beers. I went and changed my clothes and took the steins back to my cabin. I went back to the beer garden game and had a beer. After that terrible episode, I received quite a lot of sympathy from the others present at the beer garden. They said they realised what a bitch she was, and how she was taking advantage of me. They thought she was getting jealous of me making friends with other young passengers.

Friday 25th September: The *Orion* was still in the Red Sea, and turned to the east early in the morning arriving at Aden just before lunch. The *Orion* anchored out in the bay. After lunch, I went ashore by launch which cost a shilling return. I went by myself and bought my youngest brother Geoff a watch for 35 shillings. For myself, I bought a copy of *Time* magazine, and a packet of

The Orion at anchor in Aden harbour

Lucky Strike cigarettes. Having been to Aden before and

because it was so damn hot and dusty in the streets, I didn't linger in the city. I posted the letter to my family wondering if I would get home faster than me.

I returned to the ship and thought I might have a swim in the pool, but the water was too hot, 32°C. Instead, I watched the gully gully boats plying their trade, but business didn't seem as brisk as when I watched them from the deck of the *Moreton Bay* in Aden. I had a beer, sat down and read my copy of *Time* magazine, which I bought every now and again to bring me up to date with what was happening in the world.

ADEN TO COLOMBO

Distance: 2,092 Nautical miles. Steaming time: 4 days

Saturday 26th September: The *Orion* left Aden just as the sun was setting in the west in brilliant colours. We were now in the Arabian Sea and out of sight of land. It was still very hot. I had a few too many beers and got a bit drunk. Some of the young

Leaving Aden in the setting sun

Australian passengers that I was drinking and playing cards with were like me, on the way home after a grand adventure. None, however, had been away as long as me or were members of YHA.

We talked together about our time abroad and it was very interesting to compare our experiences. The young English migrants on the other hand, were facing a somewhat uncertain future, whereas I was going home to a loving family with the expectation of being able to find a job quite easily.

On the *Moreton Bay,* the swimming pool and most of the deck games and entertainment were situated directly below the bridge, within direct sight of the captain and the officers, and there was much action and repartee between us. We got to know Captain Milne when once a week he invited the passengers, in turn, to dine at his table. He was an integral part of our voyage. On the *Orion* however, I don't think I ever saw the captain. I suppose he would have been on the bridge overlooking the first-class passengers playing deck games.

Because of these differences, the social environment on the voyage home was nowhere near as enjoyable compared to my voyage to the UK. In fact, it had been a rather troubling one in many respects up to this point in the voyage.

Sunday 27th September: I woke to find we were well out into the middle of the Arabian Sea and the *Orion* was rolling quite heavily. I had three too many ice creams for lunch, so went to my bunk to sleep them off. I woke at 4 p.m. and after a few beers, I had a roaring appetite and ate my dinner like a hog. There was no entertainment after dinner, so I indulged myself again in a drinking session with the boys, mainly because I hadn't made friends with any girls on board so far.

Monday 28th September: The *Orion* was still rolling quite a lot, and I was quite excited to see some flying fish and *whales.* I certainly didn't expect to see whales this far north not far from the Equator. I spent the morning loafing and began reading the memoirs of the actress Tallulah Bankhead, a book I got from the ship's library.

Before lunch Dot sat herself beside me and said: "I am

bored." This didn't surprise me because she was not an affable person who made friends easily. I didn't buy her a beer or offer her a cigarette, nor did she offer to buy either for me. Dot looked straight at me and said: "I want to help you." How? I wasn't sure. I looked straight back and told her: "You can help me best by staying out of my way." So she did, I was pleased to say. Dot was the one who needed help I thought, not me.

After dinner, I saw the movie *Salome,* another 1953 release. It starred Rita Hayworth, Stewart Granger and Charles Laughton, quite a line-up, but nonetheless, I thought it was a lousy movie. I reckoned that *Salome* would return to the UK on the *Orion*, and wouldn't be released in Australia for another couple of years. The *Orion* was rolling so much because of a large sea swells that were running broadside to its long hull.

I went to bed as soon as the movie finished. I was not feeling 100% and as much as I hated to admit it, I think that I was a little seasick. On the other hand, maybe I had drunk too much, or it was Dot's presence that was sickening me. I consoled myself with that thought. Tuesday 29th September: The sea had flattened a little and there were a few showers. I was able to avoid Dot until after dinner, when I sat down and talked with Gerhart and Edna, a charming couple. Dot joined us and we talked together and drank gin slings. Dot bought her own and smoked her own cigarettes, which was quite an improvement, in fact, we all had a pleasant talk and drink together. I have never held grudges and am a forgiving sort of bloke, maybe I suppose because I was brought up in a Christian family.

Wednesday 30th September: The ocean was quite calm today. I played deck games and had a swim. The water in the pool was much cooler, quite invigorating in fact. After my swim I had a relaxing day reading, eating and drinking. As I relaxed I realised that tomorrow would be the beginning of my last month away from home. Approaching Colombo I looked at the dates in my diary and found that the *Orion* would be in Colombo in 4 days one day less than for the *Moreton Bay*. This prompted me to do some calculations: 1 knot=1 Nautical m/ph. Aden to Colombo 2092 N miles. *Orion's* speed 20 knots. 2092/20=104 hours or 4.3 days. The same calculation for the *Moreton Bay* with a speed of 15 knots equals 139 hours or 5.8 days. This shows how much faster this voyage was than the *Moreton Bay* especially as the *Orion* only remains in port for one day. However, I liked 'the slow boat from Port Melbourne to Southampton' much better than this troubling voyage.

Thursday 1st October: I woke to find we had arrived in Colombo in 4 days as I had calculated, one day less than the *Moreton Bay*. I went ashore by motor launch, alone because after Leon left me, I have revelled in the advantages of travelling alone, determining for myself how, when, and where I travel. I climbed aboard the red London type double-decker bus to Mt Lavinia, the same as when I went to Mt Lavinia on the way to England. I was not alone that time, I was with my happy group of canasta players. I enjoyed it so much I decided to go there again and escape the heat of Colombo. I had a tasty salad lunch and a beer in the lovely air-conditioned lounge of the resort.

I took some photos before I returned to Colombo where I had a drink at the Bristol Hotel because the Grand Oriental Hotel staff were on strike, about what I didn't know.

Passengers like me who go ashore at a port must always be sure of the sailing time before leaving their ship. Once ashore, they must ensure that there is plenty of time in reserve on any activity they take part in, so that if any problems occur there is enough time to rejoin the ship before it sails. This was especially true of the *Orion*, because she remained in port for such a short time, and left sharply on the designated hour. I made sure I was back on board at least one hour before sailing time. I saw the *Oceania,* a large liner, pull out while I was watching the gully gully boats.

I was very fortunate on both occasions to visit Ceylon in a peaceful time, because in 1958 fighting began between the Tamils and Singhalese. Violence between these two religious groups, the Buddhist Singhalese and the mainly Hindu Tamils, continues in one form or another to the present day, with both parties fighting for control of Ceylon (now called Sri Lanka).

COLOMBO TO FREMANTLE

Distance: 3.136, Nautical miles. Steaming time: 6 days

The *Orion* pulled up its anchor at 7.30 p.m. and steamed towards Australia on a very windy night. I listened to Radio Colombo and then retired to my bunk.

Friday 2nd October: The sea was quite rough and the weather squally. The service at our dining table was not very good, although the food was. We had a fancy dress ball after dinner and Dot asked me to take her. Being a forgiving person, I decided I would. We had quite an enjoyable night, although I was not a great lover of fancy dress balls. I took the easy way out and went as an Arab with a sheet draped over me and a band around my head. Dot went as a girl from a harem–not a very pretty sight, but I was sure she was oblivious of what people thought of her.

Saturday 3rd October: The weather was the same as yesterday

with squalls and rain showers so deck games were out. There was a 'housey-housey' game in the evening, but I didn't join in as I find the game boring. I was quite sure the *Orion* would cross the Equator tomorrow, but because there was no mention of any party, I thought I must be wrong. I checked the notice board and from the map of the *Orion's* progress, I was sure I was correct.

Sunday 4th October: After breakfast I went along to the stern of the *Orion* and enjoyed a favourite onboard pastime of mine, looking over the stern rail at the wake as it trailed behind the ship.

A wonerful sight, the Orion the wake and sky

I mentioned to Gerhart and Edna that we would cross the Equator today, but I did not hear any of the other passengers express any interest in the crossing, not even the immigrants from the UK, who I thought would have been looking forward to the exciting occasion. No party of any kind was organised by the ship to mark the occasion, and no mention was made of the crossing at the fancy dress ball. Maybe in first-class, the crossing was celebrated.

We had a bit of an insight into the goings-on in first class. We were able to talk to some of the young first-class passengers through a small locked gate that joined both sections on the upper deck. We discovered that the first-class passengers got all the onboard entertainment one day before us in tourist class. This was quite hilarious, because they would let us know what was coming up, and what's more, tell us some of the answers to the quizzes! There was no mention, however, of any Equator crossing party. Unlike the journey to England, I did not even bother to watch for the change in the circulation of the bathwater.

Each day was becoming a little cooler than the previous day, and the service at our table was getting worse. Our table steward would supply me and the others at our table with extra helpings of sweets and even the main course, but not offer them to the immigrants sitting at our table. Very troubling I thought. I didn't think they were being treated fairly, because they were on assisted passages.

I decided to do something about it. I sought out the dining room steward and told him that the migrants were being treated unfairly at our table and mentioned the extra helpings, which they were not being offered like us. He said he would have a word

Passing the Cocos islands

with our table steward. I didn't mention the bar service, which was not very good either. I wondered if the stewards and bar attendants in tourist class were wishing that they were working in first class, where I was sure they would be making a little extra money from tips. I don't think they were getting any from many tourist class passengers. Not from me anyhow.

Monday 5th October. I missed breakfast, but not intentionally. When I arrived in the dining room for lunch, the steward asked me: "Did you report me to the head steward?"

"I did," I replied.

He said; "One of us won't be at this table tomorrow."

I replied sternly: "**I** certainly will be. All I expect from you is proper service for all of us on this table." The steward then resumed serving us all without further ado. The others at our table were very pleased that I had taken the action I did. From that time on there was no problem, the service he gave us and the immigrants was very good, but for a while, I wondered if I would get a plate of hot soup accidentally spilt down my back.

During the day we passed the Cocos Islands, far away on the horizon. The islands are a territory of Australia. Unlike the *Moreton Bay,* we were not passed by any ships in the Indian Ocean, but the *Orion* passed a few slow freighters. In the evening I saw the movie *Top of the Form,* a good slapstick comedy. That movie was also released this year, but I didn't know any of the actors. The *Orion* was rolling heavily again. For all of its extra size and speed, I didn't think it was as stable as the *Moreton Bay*, although so far the sideboard fiddles on the dining room tables had not been required.

The young members of our dinner table the author third from the left at the back

Tuesday 6th October: Our table and the migrant lads were getting good service now without a murmur. Dot was ignoring me, which made me very happy. After dinner, I sat in a big group drinking, and then we had a scream of a time with a scavenger hunt, which I think I ended up winning, thanks to everyone's help. It was announced that tomorrow night there will be a landfall party for the tourist passengers.

Wednesday 7th October. I missed breakfast again the next morning. I also missed collecting my prize for the scavenger hunt, which was announced at breakfast. Afterwards, I was given my prize of 50 cigarettes.

The landfall party was held in the lounge bar and on tables were various hot pastries, various cuts of meat, cakes, fruit and other small items of tasty food that as I write would be termed 'nibbles,' all very tasty. Dot had kept out of my way and I was very happy and relaxed, I think for the first time on this troubling voyage. I drank beer and scotch, but kept sober and flirted with Jean, a cute New Zealander.

Thursday 8th October: There was just a gentle swell in the Indian Ocean. I didn't have a swim in the pool, it was too cold. I just loafed around the ship. We had a photo taken of the young people at our dining table. For the rest of the day, I talked to Elizabeth, an Aussie girl from Sydney. We got on famously together, talking about our time abroad. She had been away for 18 months and had hitchhiked around Europe staying in youth hostels much the same as me.

Friday 9th October: Land Ahoy! I woke to see the Australian coast on the horizon, and it was freezing cold. After breakfast, I went up on deck and was surprised to see that a tug was already ushering us into the

A shopping arcade in Perth

Fremantle wharf behind the *Himalaya* another big ocean liner.

We disembarked on to Australian soil, actually the wooden planks of the wharf, at 9 30 a.m. I went ashore with Elizabeth and a couple of New Zealanders. We went by coach to Perth on a beautiful but surprisingly cold day. Then I realised it was the middle of spring. I had a few Swan beers and a Wiener schnitzel in The Tavern. Afterwards, I went into a newsagent to buy my weekly copy of *Time* magazine. "Sorry Sir, Time magazine is only available by subscription." I had been able to purchase my weekly copy of *Time* magazine in virtually every city and town I had visited on my tours. Not being able to buy a copy from a newsagent in Perth was another example of how far Australia was behind world trends.

Back at the *Orion,* we boarded a coach organised by the purser to take us to Yanchep Park, a resort some 80 km north of Perth. We walked for about 30 minutes through the gum trees in the park, smelling the magnificent eucalyptus aroma. I knew then that I was home in Australia because we had a nice cold beer, not at room temperature. One example where Australia was ahead of the UK. Then it was time to board the coach back to the ship.

The price for cigarettes and drinks had gone up because duty was being applied here in West Australia

FREMANTLE TO PORT MELBOURNE

Distance: 1.655, Nautical miles. Steaming time: 4 days

The *Orion* pulled out of Fremantle at 7 p.m. We heard later from our first-class contacts that six first-class passengers from Sydney were left behind. They would have to catch the transcontinental train and meet the ship in Melbourne or fly. At last, I had set foot on Australian soil again. I was immediately conscious of our Australian accent when I listened to a Perth radio station announcer; "The rine in Spine stays minely on the pline."

Saturday 10th October: The *Orion* was steaming eastwards in the Great Australian Bight. The sea was rough and the weather cold. The purser said we were on schedule and should arrive in Port Melbourne in three days. That was great to hear because I had written to my mother before I left London to tell her there was a possibility that I might arrive in Port Melbourne on her birthday.

I talked again with Elizabeth and then had a sleep in the afternoon. In the evening we watched a few slides of the travels of a New Zealander. Later I had a game of canasta, my first for this voyage.

Sunday 11th October: The seas were still rough and cold and I spent most of the day with Elizabeth. We talked and played deck games together for most of the day. Dot was nowhere to be seen, I had the feeling she may have got off in Fremantle. Elizabeth was not on my dinner table, but after dinner, we sought each other out and had a drink together. If only Dot had not been around, I might have met Elizabeth earlier, and would have had a female companion for the whole of the voyage.

Monday 12th October: There was an air of excitement onboard for all of those like me who would be disembarking in Port Melbourne. I found it a little hard to relax and spent a lot of time with Elizabeth. After dinner, we had a drink together in the bar, and then we went up to the top deck. It was a beautiful clear night, not too windy or cold because we were both well rugged up. We gazed in wonder at the most wonderful starry sky that I had ever seen in my life.

The Milky Way was awesome in its brilliance. I have never forgotten the brilliance of that starry sky, which extended through all the points of the compass. I couldn't remember singling out the Southern Cross, because there were so many stars everywhere. At the time of writing, my daughter Virginia lives in Warracknabeal in the Wimmera district of Victoria where there is virtually no light or air pollution of any kind. The starry heavens above Warracknabeal however, were no rival for the brilliance and majesty of the heavens that I saw that night from the deck of the *Orion.*

I think we saw the lighthouse blinking from Cape Otway. Elizabeth and I agreed that it was a pity we hadn't met earlier in the voyage. We said goodnight and I took her back down to the lounge, where we parted with a quick kiss. I climbed into my bunk for the last time, marvelling at the heavenly vista I had just witnessed.

All of a sudden I realised that in all the time I had been away, although I had watched the emptying bathwater change direction, I had never once looked up at the northern sky to see if I could see the Pole Star.

Tuesday 13th: October 1953. The last day of my odyssey abroad. I woke to find that the *Orion* was already past Port Phillip Heads and was steaming up Port Phillip Bay with Sorrento on the starboard side. I went down to breakfast where we wished each other well and shook hands. I especially wished the young immigrants good luck and hoped they loved Australia. They were going on to Sydney. These farewells were different in kind from those on the *Moreton Bay* when we all said goodbye to each other at Southampton, where most of us were leaving the ship to begin a great adventure. Regrettably, I never managed to see Elizabeth to say goodbye.

I had my photo taken in front of the *Orion*'s spare propeller, which thankfully was not needed.

The *Orion* began edging into the wharf at Port Melbourne around noon. The noisiest people to welcome us were the six young people who had missed the boat at Fremantle. I think they must have flown to get here before us.

As the ship drew ever nearer to the wharf I saw my mother and father and my brothers Donald and Geoff. We

The author dressed ready to disembark

madly waved to each other. I had collected all my luggage by this time, and had thanked all the stewards I could see. I especially looked out our table steward and we shook hands, but I did not give him a tip.

Soon we were alongside and I was moving down the gangway to wish my mother a happy birthday and give her a big

My last look back at the Orion

hug and kiss. I think I saw tears in her eyes. I shook my father's hand and gave him a big hug. He said: "It's great to see you son, welcome home."

It was wonderful to see my two brothers Donald and Geoff and give them each a big hug. When I began talking to them, my youngest brother Geoff interrupted me and said: "Stop talking Pommy, Gordon." "I am not, I am speaking Australian."

I took one last look back at the *Orion* and took a photo of

94

her, but although she was a great ship I did not have the same affection for her that I had for the *Moreton Bay*.

Donald and Geoff helped me get my luggage off the ship, and miraculously Donald managed to get the five of us and the luggage into the car, and we began the drive home to Rosanna. I asked if we could go home along the Boulevard, just to see what our boulevard was like compared to those I had seen overseas particularly in France. Sadly our boulevard is not continuous, a couple of times we had to take side streets to join up the gaps

At last, we arrived at my dear home at 16 Hillside Road. I waved to our neighbours, who were out to greet me when they saw the car. Then into my mother's kitchen, where she quickly put on some lamb chops and fried potatoes, my favourite meal. I unpacked and got out the presents I had bought for them, while at the same time trying to tell them a little about my travels in my so-called Pommy accent.

We had a birthday cake and sang Happy Birthday to my mother, who was quite emotional, very relieved that I was home safe and sound. I received a few phone calls welcoming me home, and then we all settled down to some quiet talk until it was time for bed. I retired to my good old verandah room and soon fell asleep.

Serendipity brought about many of the highlights during my time abroad, and arriving home on the day of my mother's 51st birthday was just another serendipitous, or coincidental happening. I am quite sure she considered my homecoming to be one of her best birthday presents ever!

EPILOGUE

Most of this book was written during the coronavirus pandemic when I was isolated at home with my wife and grandson. It was also the year when cruise ships were making headlines for their part in spreading the virus.

The experiences of passengers on these cruise ships are vastly different from those I experienced on the *Moreton Bay* and the *Orion.* Both of these ships and others like them were being praised in the newspapers for their role in transporting many hundreds of migrants on £10 assisted passages to Australia, to help make Australia into the peaceful, prosperous, multicultural country it is today.

The *Moreton Bay* and the *Orion* were not cruise ships. As well as transporting migrants, they carried her Majesty's mail, freight and fare-paying passengers who had the need to travel to the UK and ports of call on the voyage for business, tourism or other purposes.

Both of these ships were of a size that the surface of the ocean was not far below the decks and the lounge bar, where most of the waking hours of the passengers spent their time during the voyage. So close that we could easily see flying fish glide above the water. Passengers could also barter and buy items offered for sale by the gully gully boats plying their trade alongside the ship while in port.

It was enthralling to observe the ever-changing waveforms of the ocean and the clouds in the sky above. Fascinating too, was the bow wave, a tangled mass of blue and white spume and spray generated by the ship as it cut its way through the sea. One of my favourite pastimes was watching from the stern railing, the ship's wake, a churned up trail of blue and white receding into the distance behind the ship.

Awesome too was the motion of the ship, whether this be pitching or rolling, or a combination of both, which most passengers were not troubled by even when in heavy seas, when the fiddles had to be fitted to the tables in the dining room to prevent the plates and food sliding on to the floor. A source of admiration on those occasions was watching how the stewards were able to serve the meals without any spills as they compensated for the movement of the ship. Passengers like me on long voyages were as one with the ship they sailed on, surrounded by the majesty of the ocean and its awe-inspiring beauty and moods.

Compare this with the cruise ships of the present day, which take tourists on short, so-called 'pleasure cruises' to many parts of the world. I have great admiration for the marine engineers, architects and workers who build these high-rise, unbeautiful, floating monstrosities.

They are designed specifically to negate most of the sensations that we enjoyed on the *TSS Moreton Bay* and *TSS Orion,* by equipping the ships with stabilisers and front end designs to smooth the bow wave. Most people who go on holidays like to get away from crowds, but these ships carrying thousands negate even that possibility. Because of the crowded, closed environment onboard, well before the coronavirus, these cruise ships have been harbingers of viruses and disease.

I am so glad that I travelled overseas over seventy years ago and not at the present time, because given similar circumstances, I would have had to endure a long flight in a metal cylinder with hardly any leg room, surrounded by many other passengers without any sight or comprehension of the lands below, and the only deck on board, the flight deck! Thankfully, the flights that I have taken were only of short duration, Scotland to Norway, Fiji twice and New Zealand, all of which were enjoyable experiences.

It is still possible to recapture the former glory of sea travel on the oceans of the world. A quick search on the internet will provide listings of many container ships and freighters that take passengers, together with the cost and voyage conditions. I have read that container ships although stabilized to some extent, pitch and roll.

And so my story of life on board the *TSS Moreton Bay* and the *TSS Orion* has come to an end, but not the memory of that wonderful time in my life when I made the big decision to travel abroad.

If the reader might wish to learn how I spent my time abroad during the two voyages I have told that story in my book *An Australian Backpacker Abroad 1951-1953.*

Email gordon.smith9715@gmail.com

ABOUT THE AUTHOR

Gordon James Robert Smith, author, historian and artist, was born in 1927 in Victoria. He went to the Heidelberg State School and the Preston Technical School, and became a tradesman fitter and turner with the Victorian Railways (VR) in 1949. He was a member of the Boy Scouts, Rover Scouts and the Youth Hostels Association (YHA). Together with another YHA member, he left Australia in 1951 to travel by ship to the UK on a working and backpacking holiday for two years. He returned to Australia in 1953. Soon after, in December 1953, he joined the SEC Kiewa Hydro-Electric Scheme and began water-colouring. In 1954 he married Dilys Terry and during his ten years on the Scheme, they raised a family of a girl and two boys

In 1963 he and his family left the SEC and shifted to Melbourne where he worked for Australian General Electric (AGE) as a facilities engineer until AGE closed down in 1983. He then taught pneumatic and hydraulics at the Royal Melbourne Technical College (RMIT) until he retired in 1993 He played golf and skied most of his life. After he retired he began writing many books about his life. He is now 92 and lives with his wife in Box Hill North.

BOOKS BY THE AUTHOR

Co-authored *Pneumatic Control for Industrial Automation,* published by John Wily. Other books by the author all self-published. *Aussie Backpacking Abroad The Beginning 1951-1953, Mountains of My Youth, Working and Raising a Family*

On The Kiewa Scheme and *Learning a Trade 1944 to 1949.* He has published the following Ebooks on Smashwords. *Two Voyages—My Journey Through Occupied Austria 1952—To the Swiss Alps via Venice—The Assimilation Of An Aussie Backpacker—Backpacking in 1952—An Aussie Backpacking Londoner—Back to Australia via France and Italy—Concrete Hard Rock Earth and Snow Part One—The High Plains Patrol—20 Watercolours of the Kiewa Scheme—An Australian Backpacker Abroad 1951-1953—Come On Board.*